SOCIAL SECURITY LEGI
SUPPLEMENT 201!

General Editor
Nick Wikeley, M.A. (Cantab)

Commentary by
Ian Hooker, LL.B.
Formerly Lecturer in Law, University of Nottingham
Formerly Chairman, Social Security Appeal Tribunals

John Mesher, B.A., B.C.L. (Oxon), LL.M. (Yale)

Richard Poynter B.C.L., M.A. (Oxon)
District Tribunal Judge,
Judge of the Upper Tribunal

Mark Rowland, LL.B.
Judge of the Upper Tribunal

Robin White, M.A., LL.M.
Emeritus Professor of Law, University of Leicester,
Judge of the Upper Tribunal

Nick Wikeley, M.A. (Cantab)
Judge of the Upper Tribunal,
Emeritus Professor of Law,
University of Southampton

David W. Williams, LL.M., Ph.D., C.T.A.
Judge of the Upper Tribunal,
Honorary Professor of Tax Law,
Queen Mary College, London

Penny Wood, LL.B., M.Sc.
District Tribunal Judge

Consultant Editor
Child Poverty Action Group

SWEET & MAXWELL

THOMSON REUTERS

Published in 2016 by Sweet & Maxwell
Part of Thomson Reuters (Professional) UK Limited
(Registered in England and Wales, Company No. 1679046. Registered
Office and address for service:
2nd floor, 1 Mark Square, Leonard Street, London EC2A 4EG)

Typeset by Wright and Round Ltd., Gloucester
Printed and bound in Great Britain by
Ashford Colour Press, Gosport, Hants

For further information on our products and services,
visit www.sweetandmaxwell.co.uk

No natural forests were destroyed to make this product.
Only farmed timber was used and re-planted.

A CIP catalogue record for this book is
available from the British Library

ISBN 978-0-414-05283-3

PREFACE

This is the Supplement to the 2015/16 edition of the four volume work, *Social Security Legislation*, which was published in September 2015.

Part I of this Supplement contains new legislation, presented in the same format as the main volumes. Parts II, III, IV and V contain the standard updating material—a separate Part for each volume of the main work—which amends the legislative text and key aspects of the commentary, drawing attention to important recent case law, so as to be up to date as at December 7, 2015. Part VI, the final section of the Supplement, gives some notice of changes forthcoming between that date and the date to which the main work (2016/17 edition) will be up to date (mid-April 2016) along with the April 2016 benefit rates.

Among the many changes, particularly noteworthy are those with respect to developments in Upper Tribunal case law relating to the descriptors for both personal independence payment (PIP) and employment and support allowance (ESA). There has also been extensive further case law impacting on the right to reside.

It should be noted that this Supplement does not seek to update the 2013/14 (first) edition of Volume V on *Universal Credit*. Extensive amendments effective up to December 31, 2014 and relating to universal credit were included in last year's Supplement to *Social Security Legislation 2014/15*, and it is planned to publish a new (second) edition of *Volume V: Universal Credit* in the course of 2016.

As always we welcome comments from those who use this Supplement. Please address these to the General Editor, Nick Wikeley, c/o School of Law, The University of Southampton, Highfield, Southampton SO17 1BJ (njw@soton.ac.uk).

Finally, this is, remarkably, the first work in this long-running series to which Professor David Bonner, formerly of the University of Leicester, has had no input. David retired as General Editor of this series in 2013, but he has continued his involvement since then as a contributor both to the main volumes and the annual Supplements. David was involved from the very outset when the series was established some 30 years ago and has now finally decided to call it a day so as to retire 'properly' and devote himself to family life, foreign travel in the Bonnermobile campervan and following (rather less far afield) his beloved Oadby Town FC (of the ChromaSport & Trophies United Counties League, Premier Division). Throughout his time with this series David has been both an outstanding team captain and team player. We will miss his drive, enthusiasm and cheerfulness as the midfield dynamo of the side. We wish him all the very best for a long, happy and healthy retirement. David may no longer be contributing to the commentary for this series, but we remain very much the Bonner Team.

Ian Hooker	Robin White
John Mesher	Nick Wikeley
Richard Poynter	David Williams
Mark Rowland	Penny Wood

December 20, 2015

CONTENTS

USING THE UPDATING MATERIAL IN THIS SUPPLEMENT

The amendments and updating material contained in Parts II–V of this Supplement are keyed in to the page numbers of the relevant main volume of *Social Security Legislation 2015/16*. Where there have been a significant number of changes to a provision, the whole section, subsection, paragraph or regulation, as amended will tend to be reproduced. Other changes may be noted by an instruction to insert or substitute new material or to delete part of the existing text. The date the change takes effect is also noted. Where explanation is needed of the change, or there is updating relating to existing annotations but no change to the legislation, you will also find commentary in this Supplement. The updating material explains new statutory material, takes on board Upper Tribunal or court decisions, or gives prominence to points which now seem to warrant more detailed attention.

For the most part any relevant new legislation since the main volumes were published is contained in Part I, while amendments to existing legislative provisions are contained in Parts II–V respectively, together with commentary on new case law. This Supplement amends the text of the main volumes of *Social Security Legislation 2015/16* to be up-to-date as at December 7, 2015.

This Supplement does not seek to update the 2013/14 (first) edition of *Volume V: Universal Credit*. Extensive amendments effective up to December 31, 2014 and relating to universal credit were included in last year's Supplement to *Social Security Legislation 2014/15*, and it is planned to publish a new (second) edition of *Volume V: Universal Credit* in the course of 2016.

Nick Wikeley
General Editor

PAGES OF MAIN VOLUMES AFFECTED
BY MATERIAL IN THIS SUPPLEMENT

Pages of Main Volumes Affected by Material in this Supplement

VOLUME II

TABLE OF ABBREVIATIONS USED IN THIS SERIES

1978 Act	Employment Protection (Consolidation) Act 1978
1979 Act	Pneumoconiosis (Workers' Compensation) Act 1979
1995 Regulations	Social Security (Incapacity for Work) (General) Regulations 1995
1998 Act	Social Security Act 1998
1999 Regulations	Social Security and Child Support (Decisions and Appeals) Regulations 1999
2002 Act	Tax Credits Act 2002
2004 Act	Child Trust Funds Act 2004
AA	Attendance Allowance
AA 1992	Attendance Allowance Act 1992
AA Regulations	Social Security (Attendance Allowance) Regulations 1991
AAC	Administrative Appeal Chamber
AACR	Administrative Appeals Chamber Reports
AAW	Algemene Arbeidsongeschiktheidswet (Dutch General Act on Incapacity for Work)
A.C.	Law Reports Appeal Cases
A.C.D.	Administrative Court Digest
ADHD	Attention Deficit Hyperactivity Disorder
Adjudication Regs	Social Security (Adjudication) Regulations 1986
Admin	Administrative Court
Admin L.R.	Administrative Law Reports
Administration Act	Social Security Administration Act 1992
AIDS	Acquired Immune Deficiency Syndrome
AIIS	Analogous Industrial Injuries Scheme
AIP	assessed income period
All E.R.	All England Reports
All E.R. (E.C.)	All England Reports (European Cases)
AMA	American Medical Association
AO	Adjudication Officer
AO	Authorised Officer
AOG	*Adjudication Officers Guide*
art.	article
Art.	Article
ASD	Autistic Spectrum Disorder

Table of Abbreviations used in this Series

ASPP	Additional Statutory Paternity Pay
A.T.C.	Annotated Tax Cases
Attendance Allowance Regulations	Social Security (Attendance Allowance) Regulations 1991
AWT	All Work Test
BA	Benefits Agency
BAMS	Benefits Agency Medical Service
B.C.L.C.	Butterworths Company Law Cases
B.H.R.C.	Butterworths Human Rights Cases
B.L.G.R.	Butterworths Local Government Reports
Blue Books	*The Law Relating to Social Security*, Vols 1–11
BMI	body mass index
B.M.L.R.	Butterworths Medico Legal Reports
B.P.I.R.	Bankruptcy and Personal Insolvency Reports
B.T.C.	British Tax Cases
BTEC	Business and Technology Education Council
B.V.C.	British Value Added Tax Reporter
B.W.C.C.	Butterworths Workmen's Compensation Cases
C	Commissioner's decision
c.	chapter
C&BA 1992	Social Security Contributions and Benefits Act 1992
CAA 2001	Capital Allowances Act 2001
CAB	Citizens Advice Bureau
CAO	Chief Adjudication Officer
CBA 1975	Child Benefit Act 1975
CBJSA	Contribution-Based Jobseeker's Allowance
C.C.L. Rep.	Community Care Law Reports
CCM	HMRC New Tax Credits Claimant Compliance Manual
CCN	New Tax Credits Claimant Compliance Manual
C.E.C.	European Community Cases
CERA	cortical evoked response audiogram
CESA	Contribution-based Employment and Support Allowance
CFS	chronic fatigue syndrome
Ch.	Chancery Division Law Reports
Child Benefit Regulations	Child Benefit (General) Regulations 2006
CIR	Commissioners of Inland Revenue
Citizenship Directive	Directive 2004/38

CJEC	Court of Justice of the European Communities
CJEU	Court of Justice of the European Union
Claims and Payments Regulations	Social Security (Claims and Payments) Regulations 1987
Claims and Payments Regulations 1979	Social Security (Claims and Payments) Regulations 1979
CMA	Chief Medical Adviser
CMEC	Child Maintenance and Enforcement Commission
C.M.L.R.	Common Market Law Reports
C.O.D.	Crown Office Digest
Com. L.R.	Commercial Law Reports
Commissioners Procedure Regulations	Social Security Commissioners (Procedure) Regulations 1999
Community treaties	EU treaties
Community institution	EU institution
Community instrument	EU instrument
Community law	EU law
Community legislation	EU legislation
Community obligation	EU obligation
Community provision	EU provision
Computation of Earnings Regulations	Social Security Benefit (Computation of Earnings) Regulations 1978
Computation of Earnings Regulations 1996	Social Security Benefit (Computation of Earnings) Regulations 1996
Con. L.R.	Construction Law Reports
Consequential Provisions Act	Social Security (Consequential Provisions) Act 1992
Const. L.J.	Construction Law Journal
Contributions and Benefits Act	Social Security Contributions and Benefits Act 1992
COPD	chronic obstructive pulmonary disease
Council Tax Benefit Regulations	Council Tax Benefit (General) Regulations 1992 (SI 1992/1814)
CP	Carer Premium
CP	Chamber President
CPAG	Child Poverty Action Group
C.P.L.R.	Civil Practice Law Reports
CPR	Civil Procedure Rules
C.P. Rep.	Civil Procedure Reports
Cr. App. R.	Criminal Appeal Reports
Cr. App. R. (S.)	Criminal Appeal Reports (Sentencing)
CRCA 2005	Commissioners for Revenue and Customs Act 2005

Credits Regulations 1974	Social Security (Credits) Regulations 1974
Credits Regulations 1975	Social Security (Credits) Regulations 1975
Crim. L.R.	Criminal Law Review
CRU	Compensation Recovery Unit
CSA 1995	Child Support Act 1995
CSIH	Inner House of the Court of Session
CSOH	Outer House of the Court of Session
CS(NI)O	Child Support (Northern Ireland) Order 1995
CSO	Child Support Officer Act 2000
CSPSSA 2000	Child Support, Pensions and Social Security Act 2000
CTA	Common Travel Area
CTB	Council Tax Benefit
CTC	Child Tax Credit
CTC Regulations	Child Tax Credit Regulations 2002
CTF	child trust fund
CTS	Carpal Tunnel Syndrome
CV	curriculum vitae
DAT	Disability Appeal Tribunal
DCA	Department for Constitutional Affairs
DCP	Disabled Child Premium
Decisions and Appeals Regulations 1999	Social Security Contributions (Decisions and Appeals) Regulations 1999
Dependency Regulations	Social Security Benefit (Dependency) Regulations 1977
DfEE	Department for Education and Employment
DHSS	Department of Health and Social Security
DIY	do it yourself
Digital Service Regulations 2014	Universal Credit (Digital Service) Amendment Regulations 2014
Disability Living Allowance Regulations	Social Security (Disability Living Allowance) Regulations
DLA	Disability Living Allowance
DLA Regulations	Social Security (Disability Living Allowance) Regulations 1991
DLAAB	Disability Living Allowance Advisory Board
DLAAB Regs	Disability Living Allowance Advisory Board Regulations 1991
DLADWAA 1991	Disability Living Allowance and Disability Working Allowance Act 1991
DM	Decision Maker

Table of Abbreviations used in this Series

DMA	Decision-making and Appeals
DMG	Decision Makers' Guidance
DMP	Delegated Medical Practitioner
DP	Disability Premium
DPTC	Disabled Person's Tax Credit
D.R.	European Commission of Human Rights Decisions and Reports
DRO	Debt Relief Order
DSD	Department for Social Development (Northern Ireland)
DSDNI	Department for Social Development, Northern Ireland
DSS	Department of Social Security
DTI	Department of Trade and Industry
DWA	Disability Working Allowance
DWP	Department of Work and Pensions
DWPMS	Department for Work and Pensions Medical Service
EAA	Extrinsic Allergic Alveolitis
EAT	Employment Appeal Tribunal
EC	Treaty establishing the European Economic Community
ECHR	European Convention on Human Rights
ECJ	European Court of Justice
ECSMA Agreement	European Convention on Social and Medical Assistance
E.C.R.	European Court Report
ECtHR	European Court of Human Rights
Ed.C.R.	Education Case Reports
EEA	European Economic Area
EEA Regulations	Immigration (European Economic Area) Regulations 2006
EEC	European Economic Community
EESSI	Electronic Exchange of Social Security Information
E.G.	Estates Gazette
E.G.L.R.	Estates Gazette Law Reports
EHIC	European Health Insurance Card
E.H.R.L.R.	European Human Rights Law Review
E.H.R.R.	European Human Rights Reports
E.L.R.	Education Law Reports
EMA	Education Maintenance Allowance
EMO	Examining Medical Officer
EMP	Examining Medical Practitioner

Employment and Support Allowance Regulations	Employment and Support Allowance Regulations 2008
Enforceable Community right	Enforceable EU right
English Regulations (eligible children)	Care Planning, Placement and Case Review (England) Regulations 2010
English Regulations (relevant children)	Care Leavers (England) Regulations 2010
Eq. L.R.	Equality Law Reports
ERA	Employment, Retention and Advancement Scheme
ERA	Evoked Response Audiometry
ERA 1996	Employment Rights Act 1996
ER(NI)O	Employers Rights (Northern Ireland) Order 1996
ES	Employment Service
ESA	Employment and Support Allowance
ESA Regulations 2008	Employment and Support Allowance Regulations 2008
ESA WCAt	Employment and Support Allowance Work Capability Assessment
ETA 1973	Employment and Training Act 1973
ETA(NI) 1950	Employment and Training Act (Northern Ireland) 1950
EU	European Union
Eu.L.R.	European Law Reports
European Coal and Steel Communities	European Union
EWCA Civ	Civil Division of the Court of Appeal in England and Wales
EWHC Admin	Administrative Court division of the High Court (England and Wales)
F(No.2)A 2005	Finance (No.2) Act 2005
FA 1990	Finance Act 1990
FA 1993	Finance Act 1993
FA 1996	Finance Act 1996
FA 2000	Finance Act 2000
FA 2004	Finance Act 2004
Fam. Law	Family Law
FAS	Financial Assistance Scheme
F.C.R.	Family Court Reporter
FIS	Family Income Supplement
FISMA 2000	Financial Services and Markets Act 2000
Fixing and Adjustment of Rates Regulations 1976	Child Benefit and Social Security (Fixing and Adjustment of Rates) Regulations 1976
F.L.R.	Family Law Reports

Table of Abbreviations used in this Series

Former Regulations	Employment and Support Allowance (Transitional Provisions, Housing Benefit and Council Tax Benefit) (Existing Awards) Regulations 2010
FME	further medical evidence
FOTRA	Free of Tax to Residents Abroad
FRAA	flat rate accrual amount
FSCS	Financial Services Compensation Scheme
FSMA 2000	Financial Services and Markets Act 2000
FSVG	Bundesgestez über die Sozialversicherung freiberuflich selbständig Erwerbstätiger (Austrian Federal Act of 30 November 1978 on social insurance for the self-employed in the liberal professions)
FTT	First-tier Tribunal
GA	Guardians Allowance
GA Regulations	Social Security (Guardian's Allowance) Regulations 1975
General Benefit Regulations 1982	Social Security (General Benefit) Regulations 1982
General Regulations	Statutory Maternity Pay (General) Regulations 1986
GMP	Guaranteed Minimum Pension
G.P.	General Practitioner
GRA	Gender Recognition Act
GRB	Graduated Retirement Benefit
GRP	Graduated Retirement Pension
G.W.D.	Greens Weekly Digest
HASSASSA	Health and Social Services and Social Security Adjudication Act 1983
HB	Housing Benefit
HCD	House of Commons Debates
HCP	health care professional
HCWA	House of Commons Written Answer
HESC	Health, Education and Social Care
HIV	Human Immunodeficiency Virus
H.L.R.	Housing Law Reports
HMIT	Her Majesty's Inspector of Taxes
HMRC	Her Majesty's Revenue and Customs
HMSO	Her Majesty's Stationery Office
HNCIP	(Housewives') Non-Contributory Invalidity Pension
Hospital In-Patients Regulations 1975	Social Security (Hospital In-Patients) Regulations 1975
Housing Benefit Regulations	Housing Benefit Regulations 2006
HP	Health Professional

Table of Abbreviations used in this Series

HPP	Higher Pensioner Premium
HRA 1998	Human Rights Act 1998
H.R.L.R.	Human Rights Law Reports–UK Cases
HSE	Health and Safety Executive
IAC	Immigration and Asylum Chamber
IAP	Intensive Activity Period
IB	Invalidity Benefit
IB/IS/SDA	Incapacity Benefits' Regime
IBJSA	Incapacity Benefit Job Seekers Allowance
IBJSA	Income-Based Jobseeker's Allowance
IB PCA	Incapacity Benefit Personal Capability Assessment
IB Regs	Social Security (Incapacity Benefit) Regulations 1994
IB Regulations	Social Security (Incapacity Benefit) Regulations 1994
IBS	Irritable Bowel Syndrome
ICA	Invalid Care Allowance
ICA Regulations	Social Security (Invalid Care Allowance) Regulations 1976
ICA Unit	Invalid Care Allowance Unit
I.C.R.	Industrial Cases Reports
ICTA 1988	Income and Corporation Taxes Act 1988
I(EEA) Regulations	Immigration (European Economic Area) Regulations 2006
IFW Regulations	Incapacity for Work (General) Regulations 1995
I.I.	Industrial Injuries
IIAC	Industrial Injuries Advisory Council
IIDB	Industrial Injuries Disablement Benefit
ILO	International Labour Organization
ILO Convention	International Labour Organization Convention
ILR	indefinite leave to remain
Imm. A.R.	Immigration Appeal Reports
Immigration and Asylum Regulations	Social Security (Immigration and Asylum) Consequential Amendments Regulations 2000
Incapacity for Work Regulations	Social Security (Incapacity for Work) (General) Regulations 1995
Income Support General Regulations	Income Support (General) Regulations 1987
Income Support Regulations	Income Support (General) Regulations 1987
Increases for Dependants Regulations	Social Security Benefit (Dependency) Regulations 1977

IND	Immigration and Nationality Directorate of the Home Office
I.N.L.R.	Immigration and Nationality Law Reports
IO	Information Officer
I.O.	Insurance Officer
IPPR	Institute of Public Policy Research
IRC	Inland Revenue Commissioners
IRESA	Income-Related Employment and Support Allowance
I.R.L.R.	Industrial Relations Law Reports
IS	Income Support
IS Regs	Income Support Regulations
IS Regulations	Income Support (General) Regulations 1987
IS	Income Support
ISA	Individual Savings Account
ISA Regulations 1998	Individual Savings Account Regulations 1998
ITA 2007	Income Tax Act 2007
ITEPA	Income Tax (Earnings and Pensions) Act 2003
ITEPA 2003	Income Tax, Earnings and Pensions Act 2003
I.T.L. Rep.	International Tax Law Reports
ITS	Independent Tribunal Service
ITTOIA	Income Tax (Trading and Other Income) Act 2005
ITTOIA 2005	Income Tax (Trading and Other Income) Act 2005
IVB	Invalidity Benefit
IWA 1994	Social Security (Incapacity for Work) Act 1994
IW	Incapacity for Work
IW (Dependants) Regs	Social Security (Incapacity for Work) (Dependants) Regulations
IW (General) Regs	Social Security (Incapacity for Work) (General) Regulations 1995
IW (Transitional) Regs	Incapacity for Work (Transitional) Regulations
JD(NI)O 1995	Jobseekers (Northern Ireland) Order 1995
Jobseeker's Allowance Regulations	Jobseekers Allowance Regulations 1996
Jobseeker's Regulations 1996	Jobseekers Allowance Regulations 1996
J.P.	Justice of the Peace Reports
J.P.L.	Journal of Public Law
JSA	Job Seekers Allowance
JSA 1995	Jobseekers Act 1995

JSA (NI) Regulations	Jobseeker's Allowance (Northern Ireland) Regulations 1996
JSA (Transitional) Regulations	Jobseeker's Allowance (Transitional) Regulations 1996
JSA Regulations 1996	Jobseekers Allowance Regulations 1996
JSA Regulations	Jobseeker's Allowance Regulations 1996
JS(NI)O 1995	Jobseekers (Northern Ireland) Order 1995
J.S.S.L.	Journal of Social Security Law
J.S.W.F.L.	Journal of Social Welfare and Family Law
J.S.W.L.	Journal of Social Welfare Law
K.B.	Law Reports, King's Bench
K.I.R.	Knight's Industrial Law Reports
L.& T.R.	Landlord and Tenant Reports
LCW	limited capability for work
LCWA	Limited Capability for Work Assessment
LCWRA	Limited Capability for Work-Related Activity
LEA	local education authority
LEL	Lower Earnings Limit
LET	low earnings threshold
L.G.R.	Local Government Law Reports
L.G. Rev.	Local Government Review
L.J.R.	Law Journal Reports
Ll.L.Rep	Lloyd's List Law Report
Lloyd's Rep.	Lloyd's Law Reports
LRP	liable relative payment
L.S.G.	Law Society Gazette
LTAHAW	Living Together as Husband and Wife
Luxembourg Court	Court of Justice of the European Union (also referred to as CJEC and ECJ)
MA	Maternity Allowance
MAF	Medical Assessment Framework
MAT	Medical Appeal Tribunal
Maternity Allowance Regulations	Social Security (Maternity Allowance) Regulations 1987
Maternity Benefit Regulations	Social Security (Maternity Benefit) Regulations 1975
ME	myalgic encephalomyelitis
Medical Evidence Regulations	Social Security (Medical Evidence) Regulations 1976
M.H.L.R.	Mental Health Law Reports
MHP	mental health problems
MIG	minimum income guarantee

Migration Regulations	Employment and Support Allowance (Transitional Provisions, Housing Benefit and Council Tax Benefit (Existing Awards) (No.2) Regulations 2010
MIRAS	mortgage interest relief at source
MRI	Magnetic resonance imaging
MRSA	methicillin-resistant Staphylococcus aureus
MS	Medical Services
NACRO	National Association for the Care and Resettlement of Offenders
NCB	National Coal Board
NDPD	Notes on the Diagnosis of Prescribed Diseases
NHS	National Health Service
NI	National Insurance
N.I.	Northern Ireland Law Reports
NI Com	Northern Ireland Commissioner
NI	National Insurance
NICA	Northern Ireland Court of Appeal
NICs	National Insurance Contributions
NICom	Northern Ireland Commissioner
NINO	National Insurance Number
NIQB	Northern Ireland, Queen's Bench Division
NIRS 2	National Insurance Recording System
N.L.J.	New Law Journal
NMC	Nursing and Midwifery Council
Northern Ireland Contributions and Benefits Act	Social Security Contributions and Benefits (Northern Ireland) Act 1992
N.P.C.	New Property Cases
NTC Manual	Clerical procedures manual on tax credits
NUM	National Union of Mineworkers
OA	Osteoarthritis
OCD	Obsessive Compulsive Disorder
OGA	Agricultural Insurance Organisation
Ogus, Barendt and Wikeley	A. Ogus, E. Barendt and N. Wikeley, *The Law of Social Security* (4th edn, Butterworths, 1995)
O.J.	Official Journal
Old Cases Act	Industrial Injuries and Diseases (Old Cases) Act 1975
OPA	Overseas Pensions Act 1973
OPB	One Parent Benefit
O.P.L.R.	Occupational Pensions Law Reports

OPSSAT	Office of the President of Social Security Appeal Tribunals
Overlapping Benefits Regulations	Social Security (Overlapping Benefits) Regulations 1979
Overpayments Regulations	Social Security (Payments on account, Overpayments and Recovery) Regulations
P. & C.R.	Property and Compensation Reports
pa	per annum
para.	paragraph
PAYE	Pay As You Earn
Payments on Account Regulations	Social Security (Payments on account, Overpayments and Recovery) Regulations
PCA	Personal Capability Assessment
PD	prescribed disease
P.D.	Practice Direction
Pens. L.R.	Pensions Law Reports
Persons Abroad Regulations	Social Security Benefit (Persons Abroad) Regulations 1975
Persons Residing Together Regulations	Social Security Benefit (Persons Residing Together) Regulations 1977
PIE	Period of Interruption of Employment
PILON	pay in lieu of notice
P.I.Q.R.	Personal Injuries and Quantum Reports
PIW	Period of Incapacity for Work
P.I.W.R.	Personal Injury and Quantum Reports
P.L.R.	Estates Gazette Planning Law Reports
Polygamous Marriages Regulations	Social Security and Family Allowances (Polygamous Marriages) Regulations 1975
PPF	Pension Protection Fund
Prescribed Diseases Regulations	Social Security (Industrial Injuries) (Prescribed Diseases) Regulations 1985
Present Regulations	Employment and Support Allowance (Transitional Provisions, Housing Benefit and Council Tax Benefit) (Existing Awards) (No.2) Regulations 2010
PSCS	Pension Service Computer System
Pt	Part
PTA	pure tone audiometry
P.T.S.R.	Public and Third Sector Law Reports
PTWR 2000	Part-time Workers (Prevention of Less Favourable Treatment) Regulations 2000
PVS	private or voluntary sectors
pw	per week
Q.B.	Queen's Bench Law Reports
QBD (NI)	Queen's Bench Division (Northern Ireland)

QEF	qualifying earnings factor
QYP	qualifying young person
R	Reported Decision
r.	rule
RC	Rules of the Court of Session
REA	Reduced Earnings Allowance
Recoupment Regulations	Social Security (Recoupment) Regulations 1990
reg.	regulation
RIPA	Regulation of Investigatory Powers Act 2000
RMO	Responsible Medical Officer
rr.	rules
R.T.R.	Road Traffic Reports
S	Scottish Decision
s.	section
SAP	Statutory Adoption Pay
SAPOE	Schemes for Assisting Persons to Obtain Employment
SAYE	Save As You Earn
SB	Supplementary Benefit
SBAT	Supplementary Benefit Appeal Tribunal
SBC	Supplementary Benefits Commission
S.C.	Session Cases
S.C. (H.L.)	Session Cases (House of Lords)
S.C. (P.C.)	Session Cases (Privy Council)
S.C.C.R.	Scottish Criminal Case Reports
S.C.L.R.	Scottish Civil Law Reports
Sch.	Schedule
SDA	Severe Disablement Allowance
SDP	Severe Disability Premium
SEC	Social Entitlement Chamber
SERPS	State Earnings Related Pension Scheme
Severe Disablement Allowance Regulations	Social Security (Severe Disablement Regulations Allowance) Regulations 1984
SI	Statutory Instrument
SIP	Share Incentive Plan
S.J.	Solicitors Journal
S.J.L.B.	Solicitors Journal Law Brief
S.L.T.	Scots Law Times
SMP	Statutory Maternity Pay
SMP (General) Regulations 1986	Statutory Maternity Pay (General) Regulations 1986
SP	Senior President

Table of Abbreviations used in this Series

SPC	State Pension Credit
SPC Regulations	State Pension Credit Regulations 2002
SPCA	State Pension Credit Act 2002
SPCA 2002	State Pension Credit Act 2002
SPCA(NI) 2002	State Pension Credit Act (Northern Ireland) 2002
SPP	Statutory Paternity Pay
SPP and SAP (Administration) Regs 2002	Statutory Paternity Pay and Statutory Adoption Pay (Administration) Regulations 2002
SPP and SAP (General) Regulations 2002	Statutory Paternity Pay and Statutory Adoption Pay (General) Regulations 2002
SPP and SAP (National Health Service)	Statutory Paternity Pay and Statutory Adoption Pay (National Health Service Employees) Regulations 2002
SPP and SAP (Weekly Rates) Regulations	Statutory Paternity Pay and Statutory Adoption Pay (Weekly Rates) Regulations 2002
SS(MP)A 1977	Social Security (Miscellaneous Provisions) Act 1977
ss.	sections
SSA 1975	Social Security Act 1975
SSA 1977	Social Security Act 1977
SSA 1978	Social Security Act 1978
SSA 1979	Social Security Act 1979
SSA 1981	Social Security Act 1981
SSA 1986	Social Security Act 1986
SSA 1988	Social Security Act 1988
SSA 1989	Social Security Act 1989
SSA 1990	Social Security Act 1990
SSA 1998	Social Security Act 1998
SSAA 1992	Social Security Administration Act 1992★
SSAC	Social Security Advisory Committee
SSAT	Social Security Appeal Tribunal
SSCB(NI)A	Social Security Contributions and Benefits (Northern Ireland) Act 1992
SSCBA 1992	Social Security Contributions and Benefits Act 1992★
SSCPA 1992	Social Security (Consequential Provisions) Act 1992
SSHBA 1982	Social Security and Housing Benefits Act 1982
SSHD	Secretary of State for the Home Department
SS(MP) A 1977	Social Security (Miscellaneous Provisions) Act 1977
SS (No.2) A 1980	Social Security (No.2) Act 1980

SSPP	statutory shared parental pay
SSP	Statutory Sick Pay
SSP (General) Regulations	Statutory Sick Pay (General) Regulations 1982
SSPA 1975	Social Security Pensions Act 1975
SSWP	Secretary of State for Work and Pensions
State Pension Credit Regulations	State Pension Credit Regulations 2002
S.T.C.	Simon's Tax Cases
S.T.C. (S.C.D.)	Simon's Tax Cases: Special Commissioners Decisions
S.T.I.	Simon's Tax Intelligence
STIB	Short-Term Incapacity Benefit
Strasbourg Court	European Court of Human Rights
Students Directive	Directive 93/96/EEC
subpara.	subparagraph
subs.	subsection
T	Tribunal of Commissioners' Decision
Taxes Act	Income and Corporation Taxes Act 1988
(TC)	Tax and Chancery
T.C.	Tax Cases
TC (Claims and Notifications) Regs 2002	Tax Credits (Claims and Notifications) Regulations 2002
TCA	Tax Credits Act
TCA 1999	Tax Credits Act 1999
TCA 2002	Tax Credits Act 2002
TCEA 2007	Tribunals, Courts and Enforcement Act 2007
TCGA	Taxation of Chargeable Gains Act 1992
TCGA 1992	Taxation of Chargeable Gains Act 2002
TCTM	Tax Credits Technical Manual
TEC	Treaty Establishing the European Community
TENS	transutaneous electrical nerve stimulation
TEU	Treaty on European Union
TFEU	Treaty on the Functioning of the European Union
The Board	Commissioners for Revenue and Customs
TIOPA 2010	Taxation (International and Other Provisions) Act 2010
TMA 1970	Taxes Management Act 1970
T.R.	Taxation Reports
Transfer of Functions Act	Social Security Contributions (Transfer of Functions etc.) Act 1999
Transitional Provisions Regulations	Employment and Support Allowance (Transitional Provisions Regulations 2008

Treaty	Rome Treaty
Tribunal Procedure Rules	Tribunal Procedure (First-tier Tribunal)(Social Entitlement Chamber) Rules 2008
UB	Unemployment Benefit
UC	Universal Credit
UCITS	Undertakings for Collective Investments in Transferable Securities
UKAIT	UK Asylum and Immigration Tribunal
UKBA	UK Border Agency of the Home Office
UKCC	United Kingdom Central Council for Nursing, Midwifery and Health Visiting
UKFTT	United Kingdom First-tier Tribunal Tax Chamber
UKHL	United Kingdom House of Lords
U.K.H.R.R.	United Kingdom Human Rights Reports
UKSC	United Kingdom Supreme Court
UKUT	United Kingdom Upper Tribunal
Unemployment, Sickness and Invalidity Benefit Regs	Social Security (Unemployment, Sickness and Invalidity Benefit) Regulations 1983
USI Regs	Social Security (Unemployment, Sickness and Invalidity Benefit) Regulations 1983
UT	Upper Tribunal
VAMS	Veterans Agency Medical Service
VAT	Value Added Tax
VCM	vinyl chloride monomer
VERA 1992	Vehicle Excise and Registration Act 1992
VWF	Vibration White Finger
W	Welsh Decision
WAO	Wet op arbeidsongeschiktheidsverzekering (Dutch Act on Incapacity for Work)
WAZ	Wet arbeidsongeschiktheidsverzekering (Dutch Act on Self-employed Persons' Incapacity for Work)
WCA/WCAt	Work Capability Assessment
Welsh Regulations	Children (Leaving Care) (Wales) Regulations 2001 (SI 2001/2189)
WFHRAt	Work-Focused Health-Related Assessment
WFI	work-focused Interview
WFTC	Working Families Tax Credit
WIA	Wet Werk en inkomen naar arbeidsvermogen (Dutch Act on Work and Income according to Labour Capacity)
Widow's Benefit and Retirement Pensions Regs	Social Security (Widow's Benefit and Retirement Pensions) Regulations 1979

Table of Abbreviations used in this Series

Wikeley, Annotations	N. Wikeley, "Annotations to Jobseekers Act 1995 (c.18)" in *Current Law Statutes Annotated* (1995)
Wikeley, Ogus and Barendt	Wikeley, Ogus and Barendt, *The Law of Social Security* (5th ed., Butterworths, 2002)
W.L.R.	Weekly Law Reports
Workmen's Compensation Acts	Workmen's Compensation Acts 1925 to 1945
WPS	War Pensions Scheme
W-RA Regs	Employment and Support Allowance (Work-Related Activity) Regulations 2011 (SI 2011/1349)
WRA 2007	Welfare Reform Act 2007
WRA 2009	Welfare Reform Act 2009
WRA 2012	Welfare Reform Act 2012
WRAAt	Work-Related Activity Assessment
WRPA 1999	Welfare Reform and Pensions Act 1999
WRP(NI)O 1999	Welfare Reform and Pensions (Northern Ireland) Order
WTC	Working Tax Credit
WTC (Entitlement and Maximum Rate) Regulations 2002	Working Tax Credit (Entitlement and Maximum Rate) Regulations 2002
WTC Regulations	Working Tax Credit (Entitlement and Maximum Rate) Regulations 2002
W.T.L.R.	Wills & Trusts Law Reports

TABLE OF CASES

Table of Cases

TABLE OF COMMISSIONERS' DECISIONS 1948–2009

Northern Ireland Commissioners'Decisions from 2010 and all Upper Tribunal decisions will be found in the Table of Cases above.

TABLE OF EU LEGISLATION

TABLE OF STATUTES

TABLE OF STATUTORY INSTRUMENTS

PART I

NEW LEGISLATION

NEW STATUTES

Pensions Act 2014

(2014 c.19)

Option to boost old retirement pensions

25. In Schedule 15—   1.001

Part 1 contains amendments to allow certain people to pay additional contributions to boost their retirement pensions;

Part 2 contains amendments to allow corresponding legislation to be put in place for Northern Ireland.

GENERAL NOTE

This section is brought into effect from October 12, 2015 together with most   1.002
of the paragraphs of Sch.15 and linked regulations. These amend relevant legislation to enable individuals to pay extra National Insurance contributions from that date to increase entitlement to state pension by making good gaps in their contribution records. This is done by creating a new class of contribution, Class 3A. The provisions relate only to what are termed "old" pensions, that is, retirement pensions payable under the law applying until April 5, 2016. There are radical changes taking place from April 6, 2016 but they apply only to those attaining state pensionable age on or after that date. The Class 3A contribution rules apply only to those who have reached or will have reached pensionable age on or before April 5, 2016 and who have an entitlement to state retirement pension under the rules applying until that date. The provisions are time-limited and allow additional contributions to be paid only during an 18 month period from introduction. Although this is entirely a matter of choice for individuals, the relevant provisions of Sch.1 Part 1 are set out below as they will in practice provide resolution for many who otherwise would not receive full state pensions. An individual can increase his or her pension entitlement by between £1 and £25 a week by paying an age-related lump sum. Details are laid down in the Social Security Class 3A Contributions (Units of Additional Pension) Regulations 2014 (SI 2014/3240) which came into force on October 12, 2015. Those regulations are not included in this work.

PART II

UPDATING MATERIAL
VOLUME I

NON MEANS-TESTED BENEFITS AND EMPLOYMENT AND SUPPORT ALLOWANCE

Commentary by

Ian Hooker

Richard Poynter

Robin White

Nick Wikeley

David Williams

Penny Wood

p.xix, *Using this Book–Northern Ireland legislation*

As mentioned in the main volume, the Welfare Reform and Work Bill that was intended to replicate in Northern Ireland most of the provisions of the Welfare Reform Act 2012 failed to pass its final stage in the Northern Ireland Assembly in May 2015 because it had not gained the necessary cross-community support. This had substantial budgetary implications because the United Kingdom Government funds welfare in Northern Ireland only up to the levels that apply in Great Britain and the 2012 Act had achieved a substantial reduction of expenditure in Great Britain. In consequence, there were 11 weeks of talks between the United Kingdom Government, Northern Ireland politicians and the Irish Government (under the approach required by the 1998 Belfast Agreement), leading to an agreement on November 17, 2015 which resulted in the Northern Ireland (Welfare Reform) Act 2015 being passed by the United Kingdom Parliament and receiving Royal Assent on November 25, 2015. It is a short statute, authorising the making of Orders in Council to make provision in connection with social security in Northern Ireland, provided that any such Order in Council is made by the end of 2016. The Welfare Reform (Northern Ireland) Order 2015 (SI 2015/2006) was duly made on December 9, 2015 and, by virtue of s.2 of the Act, is treated as an Act of the Northern Ireland Assembly. It is similar to the Bill that had failed in the Assembly seven months earlier. Most of the provisions in it will come into force in accordance with commencement orders made by the Department for Social Development. Northern Ireland legislation will then converge again with Great Britain legislation and, for instance, personal independence payment will be introduced in Northern Ireland.

p.4, *annotation to the Vaccine Damage Payments Act 1979 s.1 (Payments to persons severely disabled by vaccination)*

The 1979 Act is subject to detailed analysis in *Secretary of State for Work and Pensions v G* [2015] UKUT 321 (AAC). A child ("John") had a vaccination against pandemic influenza A (H1N1, or swine flu) when aged 7, and later developed narcolepsy and cataplexy. John's mother made a claim under the 1979 Act. Causation was not in dispute, but the Secretary of State disputed whether John met the disablement threshold of 60%. In particular, the Secretary of State argued that future developments should be discounted and John should simply be compared with a boy of the same age in normal health at the date of assessment. The First-tier Tribunal rejected that argument and decided that John's mother was entitled to the statutory award of £120,000, taking into account future disability. In a lengthy and thorough decision, Judge Mitchell dismissed the Secretary of State's appeal.

Judge Mitchell noted that s.1(1)(a) essentially set out three fundamental conditions of entitlement, namely

> "(a) causation must be established. A person must be disabled 'as a result of' vaccination'; and

2.001

(b) a disability threshold must be reached: the disability must be 'severe' and

(c) the vaccination must have been against a disease to which the Act applies" (para.44).

There are then the further conditions set out in s.1(1)(b) and (2) relating to the place and date of vaccination (in the UK after July 5, 1948), the age of the disabled person at vaccination (where relevant) and their age at date of claim (at least 2).

2.002 The assessment of disablement is governed by subs.(4), the effect of which is that s.103 of the SSCBA 1992 applies with any necessary modifications (see Judge Mitchell at paras 75–77; thus Sch.6 para.6(2) and (3) of the SSCBA do not apply—see paras 103–104). Having reviewed the principles from the industrial injuries scheme, Judge Mitchell held as follows:

"81 . . . In order, therefore, to comply with the requirement in section 1(4) of the VDPA 1979 to assess disablement 'as for the purposes of' section 103, the VDPA 1979 assessment should reflect these elements. This calls for:

(a) identification of an event akin to a relevant accident that has caused personal injury. That is if course the vaccination;

(b) identification of a loss of physical or mental faculty (or both) because of the vaccination;

(c) identification of disability or disabilities incurred as a result of the loss of faculty;

(d) a judgement to be made as to the extent of disablement, expressed as a percentage which represents the sum of the person's disabilities."

This also requires the relevant principles from Schedule 6 of the SSCBA 1992 to be imported:

"86 . . . If this is dissected, it shows:

(a) Schedule 6(1)(a) is about identifying the disabilities to be taken into account in assessing the extent of a person's disablement. Its role in the overall assessment is limited to that;

(b) the assessment is over a particular period (the 'period taken into account by the assessment') although this period is not fixed by paragraph (a);

(c) unless excluded by sub-paragraphs (b) to (d), the disabilities to be taken into account are 'all disabilities so incurred' (as a result of the loss of faculty) to which the individual 'may be expected to be subject during the period taken into account'. This requires, therefore, the assessor to make predictions about what is likely to happen during the period taken into account;

(d) in identifying the disabilities to which the person may be expected to be subject over the period taken into account, regard must be had to the individual's 'physical and mental condition at the date of the assessment';

(e) in identifying the disabilities expected during the period taken into account, a comparison is to be made with 'a person of the

8

same age and sex whose physical and mental condition is normal'."

See also, on the application of reg.11 of the Social Security (General) Benefit) Regulations 1982, Judge Mitchell's decision at paras 106–114.

Based on this careful analysis, Judge Mitchell concluded that the **2.003** assessment of disablement under the 1979 Act is not a snapshot, restricted to the presenting disablement at the time of the assessment, but rather could take into account future disability (paras 116–121). The Judge gave the following general guidance about the assessment of disablement (at para.149):

"(a) the need to identify something akin to an accident. This is straightforward because it is, of course, is the vaccination;

(b) the need to identify a loss of faculty, which is generally taken to mean 'an impairment of the proper functioning of part of the body or mind';

(c) the need to identify the period to be taken into account by the assessment. In many cases, the nature of vaccine damage is that this is the disabled person's lifetime because that will be the period during which the person is expected to suffer from the loss of faculty;

(d) the need to identify the disabilities, resulting from the vaccination, that may be expected during that period. A disability is generally taken to mean 'partial or total failure of power to perform normal bodily or mental processes';

(e) the need to understand how the prescribed scale of disablement functions and the extent to which it is legitimate to rely on it. I think it is clear that vaccine damage would be most unlikely to take the form of an injury on the prescribed scale because prescribed injuries all tend to be various types of physical trauma. Therefore, it will be used for comparative purposes only. A meaningful comparison is only likely to be made between disabilities, rather than injuries. To do that effectively calls for the disabilities associated with the prescribed injury to be compared with those associated with disabilities resulting from vaccination;

(f) the final stage in the process is to express the sum of disabilities in terms of overall disablement, using a percentage. At this stage, I think it is important to note that vaccine damage, tending often to be systemic in nature, may well result in a constellation of disabilities. These should be carefully identified;

(g) it should be remembered that personal factors may not be taken into account, other than age, sex, physical and mental condition. However, evidence about personal activities is perfectly acceptable if it says something relevant about disability or disablement."

Finally, Judge Mitchell was also highly critical of the conduct of the appeal by the Vaccine Damage Unit, in particular with regard to the poor quality of the appeal papers (paras 13, 28–29 and 145) and failure to send a presenting officer to the First-tier Tribunal hearing (para.30).

p.7, *annotation to the Vaccine Damage Payments Act 1979 s.2 (Conditions of entitlement)*

2.004   See *Secretary of State for Work and Pensions v G* [2015] UKUT 321 (AAC) at paras 42–51.

p.8, *annotation to the Vaccine Damage Payments Act 1979 s.3 (Determinations of claims)*

2.005   Section 3(1) creates a time limit for claiming by defining a claim as being a claim for payment made on or before the later of two dates, being (i) the date on which the disabled person attains 21 and (ii) the end of 6 years starting with the date of vaccination. As Judge Mitchell noted in *Secretary of State for Work and Pensions v G* [2015] UKUT 321 (AAC):

> "54. If a 'claim' is made outside this window, it is not a claim at all. The Secretary of State's duty to make a payment under section 1(1) VDPA 1979 can only arise 'on consideration of a claim'. The duty cannot be triggered, therefore, by a non-claim which is why the definition of 'claim' effectively imposes a time-limit for claiming. In this case, the claim was in-time."

p.8, *annotation to the Vaccine Damage Payments Act 1979 s.3A (Decisions reversing earlier decisions)*

2.006   In *Secretary of State for Work and Pensions v G* [2015] UKUT 321 (AAC), Judge Mitchell explained the position as follows:

> "65. Drawing the reversal strings together, the upshot, so far as unsuccessful claimants are concerned, is that, if they go to tribunal and lose, they have a limited period in which to apply for reversal. This is either two years from notification of the tribunal's decision or six years from notification of the original decision of the Secretary of State, whichever is later. But if they keep their powder dry, as it were, and do not appeal, there is no time limit and an application for reversal may be made at any time. However, the Secretary of State's power to reverse on his own initiative expires six years after notification of his original decision (unless he wishes to reverse due to misrepresentation of or failure to disclose a material fact which I imagine means converting a decision to award a payment into a decision to refuse)."

p.10, *annotation to the Vaccine Damage Payments Act 1979 s.4 (Appeals to appeal tribunals)*

2.007   Note that there is no time limit for bringing an appeal (*Secretary of State for Work and Pensions v G* [2015] UKUT 321 (AAC) at para.68). Judge Mitchell also noted that by virtue of s.4(4) the "default position" for social security appeals in s.12(8) of the Social Security Act 1988 does not apply to appeals under the 1979 Act. "Accordingly, all relevant circumstances up to the date of the appeal hearing are to be taken into account. This is consistent with the absence of a time limit for bringing an appeal because, in theory, many years might elapse between decision and appeal hearing" (at para.69).

p.10, *annotation to the Vaccine Damage Payments Act 1979 s.6 (Payments to or for the benefit of disabled persons)*

As Judge Mitchell explained in *Secretary of State for Work and Pensions v G* [2015] UKUT 321 (AAC) (at para.72), s.6(4) means that "a payment under the VDPA 1979 does not affect any rights to bring proceedings but, where civil proceedings are brought in respect of disablement, the payment will reduce the damages received by the claimant."

2.008

p.24, *amendment to Social Security Contributions and Benefits Act 1992 s.1 (Outline of contributory system)*

With effect from October 12, 2015, Sch.15, para.2 of the Pensions Act 2014 (see the Pensions Act 2014 (Commencement No.5) Regulations (SI 2015/1475)) amended s.1 by omitting "six" in subs.(2) and inserting after "making up entitlement;" in para.(d) the following:

2.009

"(da) Class 3A, payable by eligible people voluntarily under section 14A with a view to obtaining units of additional pension;".

The same amending provisions substituted ", 3 and 3A" for "and 3" in subs.(4)(a).

p.29, *amendment to Social Security Contributions and Benefits Act 1992 by addition of new ss.14A–14C*

With effect from October 12, 2015, Sch.15, para.3 of the Pensions Act 2014 (see Pensions Act 2014 (Commencement No.5) Regulations (SI 2015/1475)) inserted new ss.14A–14C as follows:

2.010

"Class 3A contributions

Class 3A contributions in return for units of additional pension

14A. [[1]] (1) An eligible person is entitled to pay a Class 3A contribution before the cut-off date, in return for a unit of additional pension.
(1A) The cut-off date is—
(a) 5th April, 2017, or
(b) If later the end of the 30 day period beginning with the day on which the person is sent information about Class 3A contributions by Her Majesty's Revenue and Customs in response to a request made before 6th April 2017.]

11

(2) A person is eligible to pay a Class 3A contribution if the person—

(a) is entitled to a Category A, Category B or Category D retirement pension or graduated retirement benefit, or

(b) has deferred entitlement to a Category A or Category B retirement pension or graduated retirement benefit.

(3) The amount of a Class 3A contribution needed to obtain a unit of additional pension is to be determined in accordance with regulations made by the Treasury.

(4) Before making those regulations the Treasury must consult the Government Actuary or the Deputy Government Actuary.

(5) A person—

(a) may pay Class 3A contributions on more than one occasion, but

(b) may not obtain more than the maximum number of units of additional pension.

(6) The maximum number of units of additional pension that a person may obtain is to be specified by the Treasury in regulations.

(7) In this section "deferred", in relation to graduated retirement benefit, has the meaning given by section 36(4A) of the National Insurance Act 1965.

(8) For the meaning of "deferred" in relation to a Category A or Category B retirement pension, see section 55(3) of this Act.

AMENDMENT

1. Subs.(1) is amended and subs.(1A) added by reg.2 of the Social Security Class 3A Contribution (Amendment) Regulations 2014, (SI 2014/2746) with effect from October 12, 2015.

Class 3A contributions: repayment

14B. (1) The Treasury may by regulations provide for a Class 3A contribution to be repaid in specified circumstances.

(2) Regulations under subsection (1) may, in particular, make provision about applications for repayments and other procedural matters.

(3) A person is to be treated as never having had a unit of additional pension if the Class 3A contribution paid in respect of it is repaid.

(4) Regulations under subsection (1) may provide for benefits paid to a person because of the unit of additional pension to be recovered by deducting them from the repayment.

Class 3A contributions: power to change eligibility or remove the option to pay

14C. (1) The Treasury may by regulations change who is eligible to pay Class 3A contributions.

(2) The Treasury may by regulations remove the option for people to pay Class 3A contributions.

(3) Regulations under this section may, in particular, amend an Act"

(4) If paragraph 3 comes into force before the day mentioned in section 56(4) of this Act, section 14A(2) as inserted by that paragraph has effect as if the reference to entitlement included the prospective entitlement of a person who—

(a) has not yet reached pensionable age, but

(b) will reach pensionable age before that day (assuming that the person lives until pensionable age).

p.50, *annotation to Social Security Contributions and Benefits Act 1992 s.39A (Widowed parent's allowance)*

The significance of entitlement to child benefit in relation to claims for this benefit is demonstrated by the decision in *GH (BB) v SSWP* [2015] UKUT 591 (AAC). There the claimant was a woman who had cared for her grandchild for all of that child's life up to the age of 13 and was in receipt of child benefit for her. At that point the child went to live with her mother because the claimant's husband was suffering from a terminal illness. This permitted the claimant to concentrate on caring for him and at the same time spared the child the experience of the final stages of his illness. The claim for child benefit was transferred to the mother. Although the child returned to live with the claimant within a few weeks of the husband's death, and intended to remain in what to her was her childhood home, the claimant could not qualify for WPA. In order to succeed she would have had to be entitled to child benefit for a child who was a child of herself and the deceased (subs.(3)(a)), or of a child in respect of whom the deceased spouse was entitled immediately before his death (subs.(3)(b)), or a child in respect of whom the claimant herself was entitled at the time of her husband's death (subs.(3)(c)). The claimant could satisfy none of these because the child was not her daughter, her husband was never entitled to the child benefit, and the claimant could not have been entitled at the time of her husband's death because child benefit was then in payment to another, namely the child's mother. Nor could the judge afford any assistance through the Human Rights Act 1998 because the limitations in question here are contained in the primary legislation so could not be disapplied. Only the High Court could consider a declaration of incompatibility—although the judge expressed doubt whether such an argument would succeed. 2.011

p.72, *amendment to Social Security Contributions and Benefits Act 1992 s.43 (Persons entitled to more than one retirement pension)*

With effect from October 12, 2015, Sch.15, para.5 of the Pensions Act 2014 (see Pensions Act 2014 (Commencement No.5) Regulations (SI 2015/1475), reg.5) amended s.43 by inserting after "subsection (2) below" in subs.(1) the following: "and section 61ZC below (which deals with unusual cases involving units of additional pension)". 2.012

p.75, *amendment to Social Security Contributions and Benefits Act 1992 s.44 (Category A retirement pension)*

2.013   With effect from October 12, 2015, Sch.15, para.6 of the Pensions Act 2014 (see Pensions Act 2014 (Commencement No.5) Regulations (SI 2015/1475)) amended s.44 by inserting at the end of subs.(3)(b) "or where the pensioner has one or more units of additional pension" and inserting afterwards: "For units of additional pension, see section 14A."

p.84, *amendment to Social Security Contributions and Benefits Act 1992 s.45 (Rate of additional pension in a Category A retirement pension)*

2.014   The amendment to s.45(1) has been incorrectly transposed in the main volume. Section 45(1) (as amended) should read as follows:

"(1) The weekly rate of the additional pension in a Category A retirement pension in any case where the pensioner attained pensionable age in a tax year before 6th April 1999 shall be the sum of the following—
  (a) in relation to any surpluses in the pensioner's earnings factors, the weekly equivalent of $1\frac{1}{4}$ per cent of the adjusted amount of the surpluses mentioned in section 44(3)(b) above; and
  (b) if the pensioner has one or more units of additional pension, a specified amount for each of those units."

p.86, *amendments to Social Security Security Contributions and Benefits Act 1992 s.45 (Rate of additional pension in a Category A retirement pension)*

2.014.1   The fourth reference to the relevant amendments should read as follows:

"4. Pensions Act 2014 Sch.15, para.7 (October 12, 2015)."

p.100, *amendment to Social Security Contributions and Benefits Act 1992 s.52 (Special provision for surviving spouses)*

2.015   With effect from October 12, 2015, Sch.15, para.8 of the Pensions Act 2014 (see Pensions Act 2014 (Commencement No.5) Regulations (SI 2015/1475)) amended s.52 by inserting after subs.(3) the following new subsections:

"(3A) In subsection (3) the references to additional pension in a Category A or Category B retirement pension do not include any amount of additional pension attributable to units of additional pension.
  (3B) If an amount of additional pension in the Category B retirement pension is attributable to units of additional pension, the additional pension in the Category A retirement pension is increased by that amount (in addition to any increase under subsection (3))."

p.106, *amendment to Social Security Contributions and Benefits Act 1992 by addition of new sections 61ZA-61ZC (Shortfall in contributions: people with units of additional pension etc)*

With effect from October 12, 2015, Sch.15, para.9 of the Pensions Act 2014 (see Pensions Act 2014 (Commencement No.5) Regulations (SI 2015/1475)) inserted the following new sections after s.61: **2.016**

"Shortfall in contributions: people with units of additional pension

61ZA. (1) This section applies to a person who has one or more units of additional pension if the person—

(a) is not entitled to a Category A retirement pension, but

(b) would be entitled to a Category A retirement pension if the relevant contribution conditions were satisfied.

(2) The relevant contribution conditions are to be taken to be satisfied for the purposes of the person's entitlement to a Category A retirement pension.

(3) But where a person is entitled to a Category A retirement pension because of this section, the only element of that pension to which the person is so entitled is the additional pension attributable to the units of additional pension.

(4) For units of additional pension, see section 14A.

Shortfall in contributions: people whose dead spouse had units of additional pension

61ZB. (1) This section applies to a person whose spouse or civil partner died with one or more units of additional pension if the person—

(a) is not entitled to a Category B retirement pension as a result of the death, but

(b) would be entitled to a Category B retirement pension as a result of the death if the relevant contribution conditions were satisfied.

(2) The relevant contribution conditions are to be taken to be satisfied for the purposes of the person's entitlement to that Category B retirement pension.

(3) But where a person is entitled to a Category B retirement pension because of this section, the only element of that pension to which the person is so entitled is the additional pension attributable to the units of additional pension.

(4) For units of additional pension, see section 14A.

Entitlement to more than one pension: sections 61ZA and 61ZB

61ZC. (1) Section 43 does not prevent a person from being entitled for the same period to both—

(a) a Category A retirement pension because of section 61ZA, and

(b) one Category B retirement pension.

(2) Section 43 does not prevent a person from being entitled for the same period to both—

(a) a Category A retirement pension, and

(b) one Category B retirement pension because of section 61ZB (or, if there is more than one such Category B retirement pension, the most favourable of them).

(3) Accordingly—

(a) in section 43(2)(a) the reference to "a Category A or a Category B retirement pension", in a case in which subsection (1) or (2) of this section applies, includes "a Category A and a Category B retirement pension",

(b) in sections 43(3)(a) and (aa), 51A and 52 "Category A retirement pension" does not include a pension to which a person is entitled because of section 61ZA, and

(c) in sections 43(3)(a) and 52 "Category B retirement pension" does not include a pension to which a person is entitled because of section 61ZB."

p.111, *annotation to Social Security Contributions and Benefits Act 1992 s.64 (Attendance allowance: entitlement)*

2.017   Note that although attendance allowance has no equivalent to the mobility component provided under DLA it is possible for a claimant who requires assistance in moving about to include that help in the assessment of their need for attention in connection with their bodily functions—in that case the bodily function of mobilising, whether indoors or out of doors. Thus, for someone in a wheelchair who requires another person to push them about, that assistance can count towards the frequency and extent of the assistance that they require; see *JB v SSWP* [2015] UKUT 361 (AAC).

p.118, *amendment to the Social Security Contributions and Benefits Act 1992 s.70 (Invalid care allowance)*

2.018   With effect from November 5, 2015, reg.11(2) of the Universal Credit and Miscellaneous Amendments Regulations amended s.70(7) by substituting "have a relevant entitlement for the same day" for "be entitled for the same day to such an allowance" and "shall have that entitlement" for "shall be entitled".

With effect from the same date reg.11(3) of those regulations inserts after subs.(7) the following new sub-section:

"(7A) For the purposes of subsection (7) a person has a "relevant entitlement" if—

(a) the person is entitled to a carer's allowance, or

(b) the person is entitled under section 12 of the Welfare Reform Act 2012 to the inclusion in an award of universal credit of an amount in respect of the fact that the person has regular and substantial caring responsibilities for a severely disabled person."

p.126, *Annotation to Social Security Contributions and Benefits Act 1992 s.71 (Disability living allowance)*

The Secretary of State's appeal to the Court of Appeal (reported as 2.019 *Tolley v SSWP* [2013] EWCA Civ 1471) was dismissed, but that decision has been appealed further to the Supreme Court. That court has referred certain questions to the CJEU (see as reported at [2015] UKSC 55).

p.156, *annotation to Social Security Contributions and Benefits Act 1992 s.72 (The care component)*

But note it is still possible to find an example where an error of law has 2.020 occurred by the application of the wrong legal test to the facts found by the FTT. In *AB v SSWP* [2015] UKUT 522 (AAC) the claimant was a person who required stimulation to her mental processes at several points during the day on about half of the days each week, although the claimant did not require someone to be with her all of the day and could safely be left on her own for part of each day. The FTT held on the facts as found by them that this qualified her for benefit at only the lowest rate, i.e. attention needed for a significant portion of the day. They held that that she did not qualify at the middle rate because, it seemed, they required the attention to have been necessary not only frequently, but also throughout the day—meaning that she might require someone to be with her all day. Judge Gray held that this was a mistake in the law as explained by Judge Hickinbottom in *R (DLA) 5/05* and that on the facts found by the FTT she was able to make the award at the middle rate without requiring a rehearing.

p.175, *annotation to Social Security Contributions and Benefits Act 1992 s.73 (The mobility component)*

The commentary on subs.(4A) has been confirmed by the Upper 2.021 Tribunal's decision in *KC-MS v SSWP* [2015] UKUT 284 (AAC). The FTT had rejected an appeal by the mother of a 6 year old child, observing that no 6 year old would be permitted to go out on unfamiliar routes without supervision. Judge Gray allowed an appeal pointing out that the test was not whether *all* such children would require supervision, but whether *this* disabled child required substantially more supervision, or a different kind of supervision, than that required by a normal child of that age.

p.181, *annotation to Social Security Contributions and Benefits Act 1992 s.73 (The mobility component)*

Note that although attendance allowance has no equivalent to the 2.022 mobility component provided under DLA it is possible for a claimant who requires assistance in moving about to include that help in the assessment of their need for attention in connection with their bodily functions in that case the bodily function of mobilising, whether indoors or out of doors. Thus, for someone in a wheelchair who requires another person to push them about, that assistance can count towards the frequency and extent of the assistance that they require; see *JB v SSWP* [2015] UKUT 361 (AAC).

p.247, *amendment to Social Security Contributions and Benefits Act 1992 s.122 (Interpretation)*

2.023   With effect from October 12, 2015, Sch.15, para.10 of the Pensions Act 2014 (see Pensions Act 2014 (Commencement No.5) Regulations (SI 2015/1475)) amended s.122 by inserting at the appropriate place in subs.(1):

> ""unit of additional pension" means a unit of additional pension for which a person has paid a Class 3A contribution under section 14A;".

p.263, *Social Security Contributions and Benefits Act 1992 Schedules*

2.024   Under the heading SCHEDULES, replace the existing text with:

> ***Schedule 1 (supplementary provisions relating to Classes 1, 1A, 2 and 3) and Schedule 2 (levy of Class 4 contributions with income tax)*** *omitted as administered by Her Majesty's Revenue and Customs with appeals to the First-tier Tribunal Tax Chamber*

p.265, *Social Security Contributions and Benefits Act 1992 Sch 3 (Contribution conditions for entitlement to benefit)*

2.024.1   With effect from October 27, 2008, s.28(1) and Sch.3, para.9(1) and (13) of the Welfare Reform Act 2007 (see also the Welfare Reform Act 2007 (Commencement No.6 and Consequential Provisions) Order 2008 (SI 2008/787), art.2(4)(b) and (f)) inserted new sub-paras (6A) and (6B) (omitted in error from the main volume):

> "(6A) The first condition shall be taken to be satisfied if the contributor concerned was entitled to main phase employment and support allowance at any time during—
> > (a)   the year in which he attained pensionable age or died under that age, or
> > (b)   the year immediately preceding that year.
>
> (6B) The reference in sub-paragraph (6A) to main phase employment and support allowance is to an employment and support allowance in the case of which the calculation of the amount payable in respect of the claimant includes an addition under section 2(1)(b) or 4(2)(b) of the Welfare Reform Act 2007 (addition where conditions of entitlement to support component or work-related activity component satisfied)."

p.349, *amendment to Welfare Reform and Pensions Act 1999 s.47*
(Sharable state scheme rights)

With effect from October 12, 2015 Sch.15, para.12 of the Pensions   2.025
Act 2014 (see Pensions Act 2014 (Commencement No.5) Regulations
(SI 2015/1475)) amended s.47 by omitting "earnings-related" in
subs.(2)(a).

p.519, *Social Security (Crediting and Treatment of Contributions, and*
National Insurance Numbers) Regulations 2001 (SI 2001/769) reg.9
(Application for allocation of national insurance number)

"Application for allocation of national insurance number   2.026

9.—(1) Subject to the provisions of paragraph (2) below, every
person, who is over the age of 16 and satisfies the conditions specified
in regulation 87 or 119 of the Contributions Regulations (conditions
of domicile or residence and conditions as to residence or presence in
Great Britain respectively), shall, unless he has already been allocated
a national insurance number under the Act, the Social Security Act
1975 or the National Insurance Act 1965, apply either to the Secretary
of State or to [the Commissioners for Her Majesty's Revenue and
Customs] for the allocation of a national insurance number and shall
make such application at such time and in such manner as the Secretary of State shall direct.

(1A) An application under paragraph (1) shall be accompanied by a
document of a description specified in Schedule 1.

(2) As respects any person who is neither an employed earner nor a
self-employed earner the provisions of paragraph (1) above shall not
apply unless and until that person wishes to pay a Class 3 or 3A
contribution.

(2A) The provisions of paragraph (1) shall not apply to a person in
respect of whom the Secretary of State or the Commissioners for Her
Majesty's Revenue and Customs are notified that a biometric immigration document is to be issued pursuant to regulation 13 or 13A of
the Immigration (Biometric Registration) Regulations 2008.

(3) The Secretary of State may authorise arrangements for the
allocation of a national insurance number to any person during the 12
months before that person reaches the age of 16, and in particular may
direct that a person who will attain the age of 16 within 12 months
after such direction shall apply for the allocation of a national insurance number before attaining the age of 16, and any such person shall
accordingly comply with such direction.

(4) Where a person—

(a) qualifies for a loan made in accordance with regulations made
under section 22 of the Teaching and Higher Education Act
1998 (new arrangements For giving financial support to stu-
dents) or sections 73 to 74(1) of the Education (Scotland) Act
1980 in connection with an academic year beginning on or after
1st September 2007; and

(b) has been required as a condition of entitlement to payment of the loan to provide his national insurance number, he shall, unless he has already been allocated a national insurance number, apply to the Secretary of State or the Commissioners for Her Majesty's Revenue and Customs for one to be allocated to him, and the Secretary of State or, as the case may be, the Commissioners may direct how the application is to be made."

GENERAL NOTE

2.027   The text of reg.9 as set out above is as amended by the Social Security (Miscellaneous Amendments) Regulations 2015 (SI 2015/67), reg.5 (with effect from February 23, 2015) and the Social Security (Crediting and Treatment of Contributions, and National Insurance Numbers) (Amendment) Regulations 2015 (SI 2015/1828), reg.2 (with effect from November 30, 2015).

2.028   **Regs 10 to 12 and Schedule** are omitted as within responsibility of HMRC and not the Secretary of State or beyond the scope of this work.

p.598, *amendment to Social Security (Overlapping Benefits) Regulations 1979 (SI 1979/597) reg.2 (Interpretation)*

2.029   With effect from May 26, 2015, art.2 and Sch.3, para.1, of the Deregulation Act 2015 (Consequential Amendments) Order 2015 (SI 2015/971) amended reg.2(1) by inserting in the definition of "training allowance" the words "the Secretary of State" for the words "the Chief Executive of Skills Funding".

p.697, *annotation to Disability Living Allowance Regulations 1991 (SI 1991/2890) reg.12 (Entitlement to the mobility component)*

2.030   The correct reference for this case should be *YR v SSWP* [2015] UKUT 80 (AAC). In *Secretary of State for Work and Pensions v Robertson* [2015] CSIH 82, the Court of Session held the further appeal by the Secretary of State to be incompetent because the Secretary of State had been successful before the Upper Tribunal: see further the note below to pp.1513–1519 of Vol.III of the main volumes.

p.725, *amendment to Invalid Care Allowance Regulations 1976 (SI 1976/ 409) reg.7 (Manner of electing the person entitled to a carer's allowance in respect of a severely disabled person where, but for section 70(7) of the Contributions and Benefits Act, more than one person would be entitled to an invalid care allowance in respect of that severely disabled person) of the Social Security (Invalid Care Allowance) Regulations 1976*

2.031   With effect from November 5, 2015, reg.12(2) of the Universal Credit and Miscellaneous Amendments Regulations 2015 (SI 2015/1754) amended reg.7(1) by substituting "have a relevant entitlement for the same day" for "be entitled for the same day to a carer's allowance"; by substituting "shall have that entitlement" for "shall be entitled"; by substituting "have a relevant entitlement" for "be entitled to a carer's allowance"; and by substituting "to have that entitlement" for "to be entitled".

With effect from the same date, reg.12(3) amended reg.7(2) by substituting "a relevant entitlement" for "entitlement to carer's allowance" and substituting "a carer's allowance or the carer element of universal credit" for "a carer's allowance".

Also with effect from the same date, reg.12(4) amended reg.7 by inserting after para.(2) the following new paragraph:

> "(3) In paragraph (2) "the carer element of universal credit" means an amount included in an award of universal credit in respect of the fact that a person has regular and substantial caring responsibilities for a severely disabled person."

p.735, *annotation to Personal Independence Payments Regulations 2013 (SI 2013/377) reg.2 (Interpretation, "aid or appliance")*

In *KR v SSWP* [2015] UKUT 547 (AAC) Judge Rowley has con- **2.032** sidered the meaning of "aid or appliance" in relation to the mobility component. The FTT had found that the claimant could move a distance of at least 50 metres and they upheld a decision to award the claimant 4 points for the mobility component under Descriptor 2b. Before the UT, the claimant's representative contended that in order to achieve that distance the claimant would require to take a puff on an inhaler and argued that this qualified him under descriptor 2c. i.e. "can . . . move unaided . . . no more than 50 metres". The question, therefore, (that had not been before the FTT) was whether the inhaler should be regarded as an aid or appliance. Superficially, it certainly appears to satisfy that definition as a "device which improves . . . [a claimant's] physical . . . function", but Judge Rowley rejects that conclusion. A distinction must be made, she says, between an aid that assists the claimant's function and a device that delivers medication that assists that function. So, as was conceded by the claimant's representative, the teaspoon that delivers a liquid analgesic could not be regarded as a device that aided the claimant's function and neither, in this case, could the inhaler. This is consistent with the advice given to the HCP in the *PIP Assessment Guide* where it is suggested (in relation to activity 3 of the daily living component) that "needles, glucose meters and inhalers are not aids" whereas "pill boxes, dosette boxes, blister packs, and alarms" that help to manage medication apparently are. No explanation is given for this distinction, though elsewhere an inhaler is described as being "medication" while a nebuliser is "therapy". The *PIP Assessment Guide* has been referred to by judges in the UT in several decisions though always with the warning that it is the view expressed on behalf of the Secretary of State only, and does not necessarily represent the law. It remains to be seen whether a device that delivers medication constantly to the claimant so as to be able to walk (such as an oxygen cylinder that is worn or carried in a sling) could be regarded as an aid.

p.736, *annotation to Personal Independence Payments Regulations 2013 (SI 2013/337) reg.3 (Daily living activities and mobility activities)*

2.033   The method of assessment for PIP is explained in some detail in the DWP *PIP Assessment Guide*. In the case of *HB v SSWP* [2015] UKUT 346 (AAC) it appears that a further stage may be involved, at least in some cases. The claimant had been seen for a face-to-face interview by an HCP as explained in that guide as part of the normal process of assessment and from which she was scored at 9 points for the daily living component and would have succeeded on her claim for benefit. But it then appears that, before a decision on her claim was made, the assessment was referred to another HCP for review. That assessment, conducted only as a desk assessment, reduced the score on 3 descriptors and in consequence the claim failed. The claimant's appeal to an FTT was refused. In the UT, Judge Wikeley allowed the appeal because the FTT had failed to explain why they had accepted the score recorded on review, rather than that made at the face-to-face interview. No explanation seems to have been offered to either tribunal for the desk reassessment. It may be that it was a part of the "reworking" procedure that is provided as a part of the Quality Audit procedure, but if that were the case some explanation ought to have been forthcoming. The FTT should have involved its inquisitorial role to elicit that information and its reasons might then have been able to satisfy both the claimant and the UT.

p.737, *annotation to Personal Independence Payments Regulations 2013 (SI 2013/377) reg.4(2A) (Assessment of ability to carry out activities)*

2.034   The meaning of "safely" in this regulation has been considered in *CE v SSWP* [2015] UKUT 643 (AAC). In this case the FTT questioned whether the definition in para.(4)(a) of the regulation precluded the concept of risk that is usually adopted in measuring safety so as to reflect both the degree of harm as well as the likelihood of harm (referred to in their decision as the *Moran* principle, from *Moran v Secretary of State for Social Services* (*The Times*, March 14, 1987, CA)). In the present case the claimant was a person who suffered from uncontrolled epilepsy, having nocturnal grand mal episodes most nights. Although daytime episodes were rare, they were still a possibility. The daily living activities of preparing food and washing and bathing, as well as the mobility activities might well have presented an unacceptable risk if the consequences of having a fit during those activities could be taken into account. But the definition provides for something to be safe so long as it is "unlikely to cause harm" and the claimant's fits occurred almost exclusively in bed at night. Judge Hemingway examined the legislative history of reg.4(2A), but he concluded that Parliament's intention is clear and the words must bear their literal meaning—a tribunal must focus only upon the likelihood of harm and reject any risk where the event is unlikely, even though the consequences may be dire. In the interests of claimants like this one the definition is very unsatisfactory, but the blame must lie, as the judge pointed out, squarely in the hands of Parliament. The legislative history is unhelpful. While both the explanatory notes to the regulations, and the Government response to consultation on them, refer to substantial harm caused, they go on to require that the harm must be likely to occur; if one were to have regard to that information when construing the regulation it might lead to the conclusion that harm had to be both likely *and* serious. That is the view taken in the *PIP Assessment Guide* in para.3.2.13, but in this respect the drafting of the regulation is clear—it requires only "to cause harm to" the claimant; the literal meaning is clear, any harm will suffice (subject, presumably, to the usual *de minimis* exception).

This case also explores new ground in relation to the meaning of the word "repeatedly" in para.(4)(b). The judge in the UT returned the case for rehearing before a new tribunal and gave some guidance for that tribunal. The evidence before the FTT suggested that the claimant's inability to cope with some daily living activities arose from the fact that after an epileptic episode she needed to sleep until late in the morning and even then, when she awoke, she was lethargic and felt dizzy, sick, weak and tired so that she was unable to do very much at all until late morning or midday. The appeal by the Secretary of State had been allowed on the ground that the FTT had failed to explain sufficiently why they were awarding some of the points that they did. In offering guidance to the new tribunal, the judge suggests that they should take a comprehensive account of the times that the claimant was so affected and then, having referred to reg.4(2A), should consider whether the claimant could do those things repeatedly and to a satisfactory standard. As he put it:

> "It seems to me it makes no sense to say a person is able to perform an activity as often as reasonably required if they cannot do so for a part of the day in which they would otherwise reasonably wish or need to do so."

The judge refers also to his own decision in *TR v SSWP* [2015] UKUT 626 (AAC), in which he had adopted the advice given in the *PIP Assessment Guide* that if a descriptor was satisfied for any part of a day (after allowing for the *de minimis* rule) it should be regarded as applying on that day. It seems that he is suggesting that a claimant whose daily routine was so affected that they could not conform to normal hours for meals, work etc., could be regarded as satisfying some of the descriptors. The difficulty with this may be to apply that approach to the words of the descriptors. There is nothing in Descriptor 1, for example, that relates to the time at which the claimant should be capable of preparing a meal, and the reference in para.(2A)(d) to a reasonable time period is only to the speed with which the claimant can accomplish a task; see the definition in para.(4)(c). It would be odd to describe a claimant who took their breakfast at midday as being unable to prepare a meal. However, note that it would not mean that every person who lies abed until late could make a claim, because for any claim to succeed it would have to be the result of that claimant's mental or physical disability and, even then, not a matter of choice on their part. It is clear that a person with this

2.035

claimant's degree of disability has a life that is seriously affected by their disability, but unless they can be seen to need supervision for their own safety and that of others, it is difficult to see how their claim can succeed.

p.739, *annotation to Personal Independence Payments Regulations 2013 (SI 2013/377) reg.6 (Scoring for mobility activities)*

2.036   An application by way of judicial review for a declaration that the Personal Independence Payments Regulations were invalid failed in *R. (Sumpter) v SSWP* [2015] EWCA Civ 1033. The applicant had argued that the consultation process that preceded the making of the regulations was unfair and therefore unlawful. In particular he argued that the threshold at which a claimant might be awarded the enhanced rate of benefit in respect of their ability to move about had been changed at a late stage of the process. The early versions of the proposed criteria had appeared to adopt the standard that had been accepted, in practice, in relation to claims for DLA as an ability to move unaided no more than 50 metres, whereas the standard adopted in the draft regulations became effectively no more than 20 metres. The Secretary of State had then undertaken a further period of consultation relating specifically to that point. In the High Court Hickinbottom J had held that, whatever might have been said about the fairness of the initial consultation, this later extension of consultation made the process, as a whole, fair (*R. (Sumpter) v Secretary of State for Work and Pensions* [2014] EWHC 2434 (Admin)). The Court of Appeal upheld that decision.

p.740, *annotation to Personal Independence Payments Regulations 2013 (SI 2013/377) reg.7 (Scoring: further provisions)*

2.037   The problem that arises when a claimant's ability to perform a task varies at different times within a single day has been dealt with in a decision of Judge Hemingway, *TR v SSWP* [2015] UKUT 626 (AAC). The claimant there had restricted eyesight such that she had difficulty in seeing in low light conditions. She had been provided with what she described as her "special lamp" to assist her in reading and she used that also when preparing meals, though her husband still needed to assist her by checking things such as whether the gas was alight, or whether things were boiling on the stove. Her restricted eyesight also limited her ability to go out at night and she would use a taxi if she needed to go to unfamiliar places. Her claim had been refused and an appeal to the FTT failed. The FTT apparently took the view that if she could perform these tasks satisfactorily "the majority of the time" her claim would fail. This may have been an application by the tribunal of the approach that has applied in claims for DLA, or, it may have been that the tribunal thought they should be applying the 50% rule applicable to the case of daily variation as required by reg.7. In the UT counsel for the Secretary of State helpfully referred the judge to the Government's response to consultation on these regulations. There, it was clearly stated that if a descriptor applied at any time within a period of 24 hours it should be regarded as applying on that day. Furthermore she referred also to the DWP Guidance to the HCP assessors which contained the same criterion in two associated paragraphs.

Judge Hemingway took the view that it was open to him to take account of those documents in approaching the interpretation of reg.7. As well, he thought that this construction was consistent with reg.4(4) in requiring that a claimant should be able to accomplish a task "repeatedly", meaning as often as reasonably required. If it were reasonable for the claimant to go out at night, for example, she should be able to do that without adopting special measures to do so. But the judge approved also two limitations suggested by counsel for the Secretary of State on this approach. First, that the inability to perform a task should be the direct result of the claimant's disability; so that, for example, where the claimant chose not to go out at night for some other reason, that day would not count, and secondly, that any inability to perform a task would be subject to a *de minimis* rule. If, therefore, the claimant's inability could properly be described as fleeting, or even just brief, this would not qualify. In particular this might cover the case of a claimant whose inability arose only until he had taken his usual medication; if the medication acted quickly and enabled the claimant then to manage tasks such as washing and dressing, they would not qualify, whereas, if the medication took so long to be effective as to mean there was an unacceptable delay in the claimant's daily business, that would qualify as an inability to perform that descriptor.

The case of *AK v SSWP* [2015] UKUT 620 (AAC) poses another   **2.038** question in applying reg.7. The claimant suffered from two independent medical conditions each of which affected his living abilities on certain days of the week. One was chronic obstructive pulmonary disease (COPD) and the other was rheumatoid arthritis. Neither disease was causatively linked to the other, but neither were they mutually exclusive; in other words, on some days the claimant might be inhibited by one or other of these diseases, on some days it might be by both, and on yet others he might not be inhibited at all by either. The evidence accepted by the FTT supported a finding that the claimant was affected by COPD on average for 3 days per week and by arthritis for 2 or 3 days of the week. The evidence accepted by the FTT supported a finding that the claimant was affected by COPD on average for 3 days per week and by arthritis for 2 or 3 days of the week. Each of these conditions affected his ability to perform various descriptors in four of the daily living activities and one of the mobility activities. The tribunal in this case appears to have assumed that the medical conditions both occurred simultaneously so that the claimant failed the 50% test (required by reg.7) on each descriptor. But would the claimant have failed the 50% rule if the medical conditions did not occur simultaneously? The FTT had made no findings that related each medical condition to the separate descriptors and the case was remitted to a fresh tribunal for that to be done.

Assuming that each medical condition, or both together, might affect the claimant's ability to perform each of the relevant descriptors it would still then be necessary to determine on how many days he was so affected. One way to do this would be for the claimant to have kept a diary of his medical conditions and how they affected him each day, but that had not been done in this case and might not be done in other cases coming before tribunals. More likely, the claimant will report, as here, an estimate of the days in each week that they are affected. Evidence on a weekly basis does not accord with the "required period" as defined in reg.7(3) which refers to the period of 3 months before (and the 9 months after) the date of claim, but it seems likely that tribunals (and others involved in this decision making) will extrapolate from the estimates that claimants can make on a weekly basis, because that is the timescale on which most claimants will think. This point was not referred to in the present case.

Assuming that the tribunal is faced with the situation, as here, where the only information available is that on some days the claimant may be affected by only one of two conditions and on other days by both conditions together, it will be necessary for the tribunal to calculate the probability that they would be affected by one, or other, or by both. This may seem a daunting task, but the method of calculating probability was supplied in this case by the Secretary of State. Using that method, the probability that the claimant might be incapacitated by one or other or both of his conditions was, in the case of rheumatism on 3 days of the week and COPD also on 3 days, a probability of 4.7 days, and if rheumatism occurred on only 2 days of the week and COPD on 3 days a probability of 4.1 days. This assumes that the each medical condition dealt with separately would affect the claimant's ability on the relevant descriptor to the same extent and both together would do the same. In that case, then the claimant would have satisfied that descriptor on more than 50% of the days in that week. If only one of the medical conditions affected a particular descriptor while the other did not (though it might have affected a lesser descriptor) then the calculation becomes much more complicated and the outcome will depend upon the extent to which each condition affects the claimant's ability in relation to each descriptor and his ability when both conditions occur simultaneously, and as well, as in this case, upon whether the rheumatism affects him on 2 or on 3 days of a week! What this does emphasise is the importance of detailed fact finding in relation to each condition, each activity and each descriptor by the FTT.

2.039   Judge Ward, in this case, has attached the Secretary of State's method of calculating probabilities as a schedule to his decision. Tribunals that are called upon to perform this exercise can read it there. That calculation produced the number of days on which the claimant was affected by one or other or both of his medical conditions. Readers of this note may find the process easier to understand if they focus, instead, on the number of days in the week that the claimant might be expected to be free of any disabling condition. If we assume that the claimant suffers from condition A on 3 days of the week, and from an unconnected condition B also for 3 days of the week, then, the chances of him being free of condition A within the week are 4/7 of the week. His chance then of not having condition B *either* in that week, are only 4/7 of those days on which he does not have A. Represented mathematically this is $4/7 \times 4/7 = 16/49$ of a week, or $16/49 \times 7 = 2.3$. The claimant would be expected to have 2.3 days in a week on which he suffered no disability and, therefore 4.7 days on which he did.

One further point should be noted. In order to satisfy the 50% rule prescribed in reg.7 the probability (expectation value) shown by this calculation will have to be greater than 3.5—reg.7 requires "over 50% of the days", but what if the result is more than 3 though less than 3.5. Can the claimant then argue that by applying the "any part of a day" rule exemplified above, he should then have the days' of disablement rounded up to 4? The answer is no. To do that would amount to "double counting" because the part-day rule will have already been employed in identifying the days on which the claimant is affected by each of his conditions. The calculation of the probabilities is then purely an exercise in statistics.

p.757, *correction to Personal Independence Payments Regulations 2013 (SI 2013/377) Sch.1 (Interpretation, "monitor health")*

The words "without which C's health is likely to deteriorate;" in the last line of this definition should be indented so as to apply only to subparas (i)–(iii) of para.(b) of this definition. They do not condition para.(a).

2.040

p.763, *annotation to Personal Independence Payments Regulations 2013 (SI 2013/377) Sch.1 para.1 (General note—Interpretation)*

The meaning of "aid or appliance" has been considered by Judge Mark in *NA v SSWP* [2015] UKUT 572 (AAC). There, the claimant had been found to require the use of a perching stool when preparing a meal and of a chair when taking a shower or bath, but the FTT had not allowed any points in relation to Activity 6, dressing and undressing. The claimant had said that she could dress and undress by sitting on a chair; the FTT evidently took the view that using a chair when dressing and undressing was not the use of an aid or appliance. Judge Mark held that it could be and the fact that a chair might have some other primary purpose, did not mean that it could not be a "device which improves" the claimant's physical function in accordance with the definition of an aid in reg.2. The fact that able people might also use a chair in that manner was not the point; the question to be answered was whether the claimant could dress etc. without using such a chair.

2.041

Note that the Department of Work and Pensions has published a consultation paper entitled "Personal Independence Payment: aids and applicances descriptors" in December 2015. The consultation paper is avilable at *http://www.gov.uk/government/consultations/personal-independence-payment-aids-and-applicances-descriptors.* Consultation closed at the end of January 2016. Further amendment to the regulations is to be expected.

p.764, *annotation to Personal Independence Payments Regulations 2013 (SI 2013/377) Sch.1 (Daily Living Component, Activity 1—Preparing food)*

2.042   In *RH v SSWP* [2015] UKUT 281 (AAC) an appeal by the Secretary of State was allowed when the FTT had awarded 2 points under this descriptor because the claimant could not bend down to use the oven. It appears that the FTT had overlooked the definition of "cook" in art.1 of the schedule, meaning to heat food at or above waist height. Given that most claimants' "conventional cooker" will provide only a low level oven this means that cooking a meal may have to be accomplished without the use of an oven. The judge does anticipate problems in identifying what is meant by a conventional cooker (compare with DLA where the term used was a traditional cooker). In practice this is likely to be taken as the cooker that is currently available to the claimant. If that cooker is for some reason unusable by them (e.g. the claimant is allergic to gas, or has a phobia about the use of gas) the only issue that could arise would be whether it was reasonable to expect the claimant to replace that cooker with another one—possibly a microwave. (See below and also reg.4(2A)).

The use of a chair or stool (a so-called perching stool) in the kitchen to assist a claimant whose condition restricted the amount of time for which they could stand, has long been accepted in relation to claims for DLA—so too then, for PIP, it has been accepted in *EG v SSWP* [2015] UKUT 275 (AAC) and is referred to specifically in the *PIP Assessment Guide*. In fact this case goes further for Judge Wright accepts, though without the benefit of full argument, that the same might be said of a walking stick, if that were used by the claimant to improve their steadiness in the kitchen. This might be especially so (with regard to reg.4(2A)) where, without a stick, the claimant would be in danger of falling.

2.043   It has been held, in *GB v SSWP* [2015] UKUT 546 (AAC) that a lever-arm type tap fitted in the claimant's kitchen was an aid or appliance used in preparing food. The judge held that cooking and preparing food were separate processes, but the use of such a tap in connection with the preparation of food alone would suffice to for the purpose of this descriptor. This point might be unimportant in this case as one could hardly cook certain foods without adding water, but there will be other devices whose use applies only in preparation and not in cooking. The FTT had rejected this part of the claim though it is not clear whether that was because they found that the tap could not be an aid or appliance, or whether they thought that this claimant did not need the aid. The case was returned for rehearing on this and other points. It might be noted, as did the judge, that use of lever type taps is specified as an aid or appliance in the *PIP Assessment Guide*. Presumably if the claimant needs such taps in the kitchen he could equally be shown to have a similar need in the bathroom.

In *AM v SSWP* [2015] UKUT 215 (AAC) Judge Mark dealt with a case concerning a claimant who suffered from Asperger's Syndrome and from OCD (obsessive compulsive disorder). When following a recipe those conditions compelled him to cook each ingredient separately with the effect that any meal he prepared became inedible. The FTT had awarded him 4 points under Descriptor 1e on the ground that he needed someone to assist him in cooking the meal. The Secretary of State had appealed against this finding on the ground that only an award under Descriptor 1d would be appropriate, because what seemed to be called for was prompting, rather than assistance. Judge Mark said the FTT had failed to explain the reason for preferring the higher score, but in the event this error did not matter because the claim succeeded on other grounds.

p.766, *annotation to Personal Independence Payments Regulations 2013 (SI 2013/377) Sch.1 (Daily Living Component, Activity 2—Taking nutrition)*

In *SA v SSWP* [2015] UKUT 512 (AAC) Judge Mark has considered the case of the case of a woman who had a loss of appetite and lacked motivation to either prepare food or to eat it. She stayed with her daughter 4 days of the week where she could share the meal cooked by her daughter, though still then only with encouragement; the rest of the week she lived on soup and coffee and sometimes a sandwich. The FTT had found that although she lacked motivation to prepare food, that when it was provided for her, she could take food without assistance and refused to award any points. The UT reinstated the 4 points that had been awarded by the HCP. The judge observed that no attention had been given by the tribunal to the number of days on which the claimant needed assistance, and that the FTT appeared to have confused her lack of motivation to prepare food with her reluctance to eat. On the evidence found by the FTT it required encouragement from her daughter to do so even on the days when a meal had been prepared for her. As this was more than 50% of the days in a week that alone was sufficient to qualify under descriptor 2b, but the judge seems to suggest also that the diet followed on the other 3 days, of soup and coffee etc, was not to be regarded as a satisfactory diet. "Nutrition" is not defined in the regulation, but this suggests that there might be some minimal level of food value necessary to constitute nutrition. 2.044

p.766, *annotation to Personal Independence Payments Regulations 2013 (SI 2013/377) Sch.1 (Daily Living Component, Activity 3—Managing therapy or monitoring a health condition)*

A broad view of the meaning of "manage therapy" has been taken in *RH v SSWP* [2015] UKUT 281 (AAC). The claimant used a TENS (transcutaneous electrical nerve stimulation) machine daily for the relief of pain and required his wife to spend 10 minutes each morning helping him to fit it, and 2 minutes each night helping to remove it. The claimant had argued that this meant he required assistance throughout the day to manage his therapy. The FTT took the view that it was the machine that 2.045

managed his therapy; fitting and removal did not constitute assistance with that. The UT allowed an appeal on the basis, agreed by the Secretary of State, that such help was assistance in managing his therapy though only for less than 3.5 hours per day and therefore satisfied only Descriptor 3c. The claimant's argument depended upon an ambiguity that is inherent in the drafting of the last four paragraphs of this activity. Each refers to "supervision etc to . . . manage therapy that takes no more than" a specified time each week. The question is—does the time specified refer to the duration of the supervision etc, or does it refer to the duration of the therapy? As drafted, the more grammatical construction might be the latter. In this case the judge, without really adverting to the point, prefers the former.

The same point has been considered fully by Judge Williams in two cases, *JT v SSWP* [2015] UKUT 554 (AAC) and *HH v SWP* [2015] UKUT 558 (AAC). In the second case the claimant was a person who required renal dialysis several times every day. It was accepted that he required assistance in using the equipment and in monitoring the process, but for relatively short periods each week. It was only if the descriptor was interpreted as referring to the duration of the therapy that the claimant could score sufficient points to qualify for this component. Judge Williams refers to the definition of therapy which involves the prescription or recommendation by a health professional to deduce that it must be the supervision that is to be measured in time. This may be so, but there will be many cases where the therapy, once prescribed or recommended by the health professional, is administered solely by a friend or member of the family. Judge Williams refers also, in the first case, to the interpretation that is suggested in the *PIP Assessment Guide* where it illustrates the point by referring to the time taken to apply and to remove bandages and not to the time for which the bandage is worn. He warns though, that the *Guide* is only an expression of the view taken by the Secretary of State and is not determinative of the law.

2.046 The first of these cases reveals further problems with the drafting of these descriptors, some of which do not emerge from the judgments given. The activity envisages that there will be a distinction between "medication" and "therapy" because each term is defined separately in reg.2 and some descriptors cover both medication and therapy, while others refer either to medication or to therapy. The definitions themselves are not helpful because rather than define what is meant by either word they have the effect only of confining any medication or therapy to that which has been prescribed or recommended by a health professional. The meaning of both "medication" and "therapy" is left to the tribunal, probably with recourse to a dictionary and the experience of the tribunal members. The importance of understanding the use of each term is brought out by the facts of *JT v SSWP* [2015] UKUT 554 (AAC). The claimant suffered from a condition that necessitated daily use of a dilator to maintain the function of her urethra. She used this device herself for about an hour each day at home in the evening. Clearly the dilator was an "aid" and its use would seem to constitute managing therapy rather than medication. The claimant could not, therefore, manage her therapy "unaided" but neither subparagraph of Descriptor

3b seems applicable because subpara.(i) refers only to managing medication, while subpara.(ii) relates only to supervision, prompting or assistance, and in this case the claimant managed the therapy for herself. Nor could she satisfy any of the remaining descriptors because none of them refers to the use of an aid. This meant that the claimant was forced to argue that she needed supervision, prompting or assistance to manage her therapy, which would have scored 4 points under Descriptor 3c. The judge appears to have accepted (perhaps just for the sake of argument) the claimant's argument that the prescribing and recommendation by her doctor and advice from a nurse, could amount to the necessary supervision, prompting or assistance, but of these, supervision and assistance are defined para.1 of the Schedule so as to require the presence of the person supervising or assisting which did not appear to be the case here, and neither did it appear that the claimant required any prompting. It appears, therefore, that the only way this claimant could have scored even 1 point would be if her use of the dilator could be regarded as "managing medication" with use of an aid.

In *PC v SSWP* [2015] UKUT 622 (AAC) it has become apparent that some treatments might be regarded as both medication and as therapy. In that case the claimant suffered from eczema for which she was prescribed an emollient cream by her doctor. She also suffered from what was probably arthritis that made it difficult for her to reach parts of her body to which she needed to apply the cream—to do that, she needed assistance from another person. The FTT had awarded points under Descriptor 3b, but they did so on a completely different basis —needing an aid to manage her tablets. With regard to the cream they had made no finding at all. The question that now arose before the UT was whether the rubbing on of the cream should be regarded as "managing therapy" and thus qualifying the claimant under Descriptor 3c. The judge took the view that it might so qualify, but that, a determination of the matter, was best left to the expertise that would be available in the new tribunal to whom the case was referred on this and other grounds. If applying a therapeutic cream can constitute managing therapy, then perhaps manipulating a dilator can be managing medication.

p.767, *annotation to Personal Independence Payments Regulations 2013 (SI 2013/377) Sch.1 (Daily Living Component, Activity 5—Managing toilet needs or incontinence)*

In the case of *GP v SSWP* [2015] UKUT 498 (AAC) Judge Hemingway has dealt with the question whether a difficulty in dressing and undressing could count for both Activity 6 and for this activity when it was necessary for the claimant to remove and replace clothing when using the toilet. He held that it does not, but not because, as argued by the representative of the Secretary of State, that to do so would amount to "double counting"—he observes that the same disability will frequently entitle a claimant to score under more than one activity. The reason why dressing and undressing does not count here, is because of the way that "toilet needs" and "managing incontinence" are defined in

2.047

Pt 1 of this Schedule. Each is defined in such a way that the process of undressing and dressing does not form part of that activity—hence no points can be scored in respect of difficulty in doing so.

The decision in *GW v SSWP* [2015] UKUT 570 (AAC) also explains the meaning of "toilet needs" as defined in Pt 1 of the Schedule. There, getting on and off the toilet, evacuating bowels and bladder, and cleaning oneself afterwards, are all linked by the conjunction "and". In the FTT it was held that this meant that a claimant must be unable to accomplish all three parts of this definition before they could qualify for 2 points under Descriptor 5b. In the UT Judge Rowley held that this was wrong. In this context, she said, the word was used disjunctively and hence an inability to accomplish any one of these parts would qualify. In this case the claimant was an obese man. He had been allowed points under both Activity 4 (Washing and bathing) and under Activity 6 (Dressing and undressing) because he needed to use an aid to assist in those functions. In the toilet he needed to use a shower head or brush to clean himself and so was awarded 2 points under this descriptor also.

2.048   The decision in *JT v SSWP* [2015] UKUT 554 (AAC) deals with a possible relationship between this activity and Activity 3 (Managing therapy etc). The claimant in that case needed to use a dilator on a daily basis in order to maintain the use of her urethra—if she did not do so she would need to undergo surgery to reopen the urethra and permit her to evacuate her bladder. It did not appear from the evidence recorded that she used the dilator when actually using the toilet, but her claim seems to have been based on the argument that she needed to use an aid (the dilator) to manage her toilet needs—Descriptor 5b. The FTT had rejected her claim on the basis that they did not see a sufficiently direct connection between the use of the dilator and the use of the toilet, but they seem also to have taken the view that because the claimant's use of the dilator was pertinent in relation to Activity 3, it could not be considered, as well, in relation to Activity 5. Judge Williams allowed an appeal and returned the case for consideration by a fresh tribunal. In doing so he deals first with this point about overlap between the activities. As he puts it, simply because a particular disability is relevant in relation to one activity is no reason why it should not apply also to another—there will be numerous cases where upper body disabilities or mental disabilities affect several activities. What was not clear, and was why the judge returned the case to another tribunal, was whether the claimant did, at the relevant time, have to use a catheter to empty her bladder, or to use incontinence pads, both of which would be aids or appliances that she used to manage toiletry needs. But the real question in this case is, if the dilator is used only as device that will subsequently facilitate the passing of urine, as and when that may be necessary, can it be said to be used to manage toiletry needs? There must be some point at which the management of a condition relates to the medical treatment of the claimant, rather to the management of their toiletry needs otherwise the surgery that the claimant had undergone, on at least two occasions, would be "assistance" in managing her toiletry needs. It was only the daily repetition of the dilation procedure that might seem to make it a part of her toileting management.

p.767, *annotation to Personal Independence Payments Regulations 2013 (SI 2013/377) Sch.1 (Daily Living Component, Activity 6—Dressing and undressing)*

In *NA v SSWP* [2015] UKUT 572 (AAC) Judge Mark held that the   2.049
claimant's use of a chair, or a bed, to dress and undress could satisfy
Descriptor 6b. It mattered not that able people might similarly use a
chair or bed to dress or to help put on their shoes; what mattered was
whether the claimant was *unable* to do those things without that aid to
assist them.

The meaning of "dressing" has been explored by Judge Jacobs in *PE
v SSWP* [2015] UKUT 309 (AAC). The claimant had failed in her
claim because although in her claim pack she had stated that she needed
help when dressing, when before the FTT, she said that she managed to
dress by wearing "easy to wear" clothing. The judge allowed her appeal
on the basis that the test in Activity 6 was based upon a abstract test of
normal clothing which the representative of the Secretary of State
appears to have accepted means 'clothing which is appropriate to the
general norms of society at large.' In this case she argued the FTT had
clearly found that the claimant's "easy to wear" clothing was appropriate. The judge returned the case for rehearing. In his view just as a
claimant could not elevate their degree of disability by insisting on
wearing clothes that were particularly difficult to manage, so too, they
would not be required to reduce their disability by wearing only loose
fitting and elasticated clothes. The judge suggested that the new tribunal
should focus first upon the ways in which the claimant's disability
affected her ability to dress—bending, reaching and twisting together
with any degree of pain associated with the process. They should also
consider the effect that reg.4(2A) might have in assessing her ability to
do so to an acceptable standard and within a reasonable time.

In this case it does not appear that the judge had been referred to the
PIP Assessment Guide as has been done in other cases. Although the *Guide*
is not determinative of meaning in the regulations it has been accepted
as helpful in interpreting them. The judge might have found helpful the
first paragraph relating to Activity 6 which reads as follows:

> "This activity assesses a claimant's ability to put on and take off
> culturally appropriate, un-adapted clothing that is suitable for the
> situation. This may include the need for fastenings, such as zips or
> buttons and considers the ability to put on/take off socks and
> shoes."

p.768, *annotation to Personal Independence Payments Regulations 2013
(SI 2013/377) Sch.1 (Daily Living Component, Activity 9—Engaging
with other people face to face)*

A decision of Judge Mark *PR v SSWP* [2015] UKUT 584 (AAC) has   2.050
clarified two points in applying this descriptor. First, the definition in
para.1 of this Schedule of "social support" as support from a person
"trained or experienced in assisting people to engage in social situations"
might reasonably have been thought to include only those people who

have had training or experience in handling this situation for people in general, but this case establishes that it will suffice if the person assisting does so in light of experience only of that particular claimant. This means that assistance from family members and friends will qualify as social support. This was pointed out by the representative of the Secretary of State as having been explained in the Government's response to consultation on the assessment guide and is now contained in the *Guide* itself. The second point made by Judge Mark is that for social support to be given, does not require that the assistant is there at the time of engaging face to face; the support may be given by counselling beforehand, but without which, the claimant would be unable to engage with other people. Indeed, the *PIP Assessment Guide* goes even further—it points out that the claimant may not have support at all—what is required is that the claimant *needs* social support and that may be the case even when none has been provided.

In *AM v SSWP* [2015] UKUT 215 (AAC) Judge Mark has upheld the decision of an FTT that awarded benefit to a claimant who suffered from both Asperger's Syndrome and from OCD (obsessive compulsive disorder). The judge held that while they may have failed to give sufficient reasons for one part of their decision (see Activity 1, above) this would make no difference to the outcome of the case. In upholding the decision in respect of Activity 9, an award of 8 points under Descriptor 9d, the judge found no mistake. He did, though, point up some difficulties with the wording of this activity. First, although para.1 of this Schedule contains a definition of "engage socially" that expression does not appear in this activity or, indeed, anywhere else in the Schedule. But that definition does serve to identify the factors that might be involved in measuring a claimant's ability to engage effectively. More problematically, there may be difficulty in reconciling the requirements under reg.4(2A) for the claimant to engage with other people safely and to an acceptable standard, and for the need in Descriptor 9d for the claimant to do so without overwhelming psychological distress or causing a substantial risk of harm. If the evidence shows that the claimant cannot (on more than 50% of the days in the relevant period) engage safely and to a satisfactory extent is it necessary to find, as well, that the same behaviour shows the necessary overwhelming distress and risk to safety? In the view of Judge Mark it was sufficient for the tribunal to have found, on the evidence that was before them, that the claimant could not engage socially safely and to an acceptable extent; it was not necessary for them then to make a separate finding that this was because of overwhelming psychological distress or the risk of substantial harm. Perhaps the best explanation is that the same evidence fulfilled both requirements.

p.769, *annotation to Personal Independence Payments Regulations 2013, (SI 2013/377) Sch.1 Pt 3 (Mobility Activities, Activity 1—Planning and following journeys)*

2.051   In *SS v SSWP* [2015] UKUT 240 (AAC) Judge Wikeley has addressed the question of whether an eye patch worn by a person to assist their vision should be regarded as an "aid", or even possibly an "orientation aid" in relation to this activity. It was unnecessary for him to decide the point because the Secretary of State's appeal against an award of benefit was dismissed as involving no error of law, but in the judge's opinion an eye patch might very well qualify either as an aid or an orientation aid, if, by wearing it, the claimant were then able, with improved vision or concentration, to follow a route either planned or unplanned. The judge observed that it would depend too, on whether the claimant in fact used an eyepatch and, if not, whether it was reasonable for him to do so having regard to any medical advice that he might have been given. In the case before him the claimant had suffered extreme pain from light in one eye (the other apparently had normal vision) which affected his ability to concentrate and to follow a route.

Two cases have been reported that involve claimants who, through suffering from depression and anxiety, have claimed the mobility component on the ground that they are unable to go out and to follow a route on their own. The first, a decision of Judge Jacobs, is *DA v SSWP* [2015] UKUT 344 (AAC). The claimant reported that she suffered anxiety and distress when she went out, to the point that she avoided going out unless really necessary and that when she did so, she avoided contact with other people. The FTT that heard her appeal allowed her 4 points under the daily living component (Activity 9) on the ground that she needed social support when engaging with other people. Permission to appeal to the UT was given on the ground that the tribunal may have overlooked the fact that similar help might be needed if the claimant were to attempt an unfamiliar journey because, in the event of her becoming lost or diverted, she would need to communicate with other people in order to regain the route and that this raised a question of law as to whether such assistance from others meant that the claimant was unable to follow an unfamiliar route on her own (Descriptor 1d). Judge Jacobs held that to "follow" a route did not involve interaction with other people. In his view following a route involves only the process of navigation; it does not extend to dealing with incidents that may arise along that route. Such interaction, when necessary, would relate to the matter of "undertaking" a journey and that condition applied separately under different descriptors of this activity. In his view the contrast of language in each descriptor between "planning", "following" and "undertaking" was deliberate and meaningful; distress and anxiety of the kind demonstrated here might relate to undertaking a journey, but to result in a qualifying score it would need to involve overwhelming psychological distress to the claimant.

In the other case, *RC v SSWP* [2015] UKUT 386 (AAC), the judge has taken a different view of the matter. There, it was said that the claimant's anxiety and distress was such that without prompting and without the company of another person she did not go out at all. Judge Sir Crispin Agnew held that Descriptor 1d should not be limited only to the function of following a route, but that it should be read as including a claimant who, though capable of navigating, could not go out at all without another person. In other words, in his view, a person who cannot go out at all without company, cannot follow the route of a journey and qualifies under Descriptor 1d. The trouble with this argument is that it

2.052

35

does not then make any distinction between an unfamiliar route and a familiar one—the person who is inhibited from going at all, will need company even on a familiar route. This means that the claimant then qualifies under Descriptor 1f for 12 points and for benefit at the higher rate, when the descriptor that has plainly been intended to pick up the case of an agoraphobic, is Descriptor 1e with only 10 points and the standard rate of benefit.

The conflict between *DA v SSWP* and *RC v SSWP* in respect of the test "follow the route of a journey" in mobility Descriptors 1d and 1f may be addressed in UK/313/2015 (PIP); CPIP/1849/2015; CPIP/1347/2015, currently before the Upper Tribunal. The issue in those appeals is whether those descriptors are limited to sensory and cognitive impairment and whether psychological impairment can amount to cognitive impairment in that context.

p.770, *annotation to Personal Independence Payments Regulations 2013 (SI 2013/377) (Mobility Activities, Activity 2—Moving around)*

2.053   In *KR v SSWP* [2015] UKUT 547 (AAC) Judge Rowley had to consider whether an inhaler used by a claimant who suffered from asthma was an "aid" when used to achieve movement to a prescribed extent. Judge Rowley decided that it was not and instructed a new tribunal, to whom the case was returned, to approach the matter on that basis. She found that the inhaler should be regarded as a device that delivered medicine only and that it was the medicine, rather than the device, that improved the claimant's ability to walk. It was, she held, consistent with the approach adopted throughout the benefit system that the claimant should be assessed with the advantage of the medicine that they did take or any medicine that it was reasonable to expect them to take. (For a more general discussion of the meaning of aid or appliance see the notes following reg.2 of these regulations).

There are now two conflicting decisions on the interpretation of Descriptor 2c. This is important because that descriptor awards 8 points—sufficient to qualify the claimant at the standard rate for the mobility component. The application of Activity 2 was always going to be difficult. Reading Descriptor 2c literally, a person who could move more than 20 but no more than 50 metres unaided, satisfies that descriptor and that could be said to be the case even if, with an aid or appliance, they could then progress a further 1000 metres! That was the meaning accepted originally in the commentary to this descriptor, but is now questioned because if this descriptor is given its literal meaning it then makes nonsense of Descriptor 2a because that descriptor says a claimant who can move more than 200 metres *aided or unaided* scores nothing. This was the argument put to Judge Hemingway in *JP v SSWP* [2015] UKUT 529 (AAC) by the Secretary of State's representative. As he put it, a claimant who could walk more than 200 metres, but only with the aid of a stick or other appliance used for the *whole* of that journey, would be treated less favourably that one who could walk up to 50 metres unaided and could then carry on indefinitely with the aid of a stick— arguably the former person was the more disabled and therefore more deserving. He suggests that, reading Descriptor 2c in the context of all the other descriptors, it (and 2d) must be read as applying only to a person who can move up to 50 metres with an aid, but then can move no further at all. (The difference between 2c (8 points) and 2d (10 points) then depends upon whether the claimant can do that unaided or only with an aid). Note that if the claimant in *KR v SSWP* (above) was able to walk beyond 50 metres with the aid of his inhaler that case could have been disposed of on this basis too.

This interpretation of Descriptor 2c has been rejected in *KL v SSWP* [2015] UKUT 612 (AAC) by Judge Mitchell. In this case the claimant had a condition of her ankle which required her to use a crutch or walking stick. With that aid she could walk more than 200 metres. It does not appear from the evidence whether, without an aid, she could move at all. The FTT to whom she had appealed rejected that appeal applying the words of Descriptor 2a, "can stand and move more than 200 metres aided or unaided". They did not consider her ability to move unaided and hence did not refer to Descriptor 2c. Judge Mitchell finds that it was an error to do so and referred the case back for rehearing. The argument made in the case above, *JP v SSWP,* was not put to the judge in this case, but he refers to it on the basis that it might well be put before the new FTT on rehearing. In his view the logic, or lack of it, in the construction of this activity and the descriptors provided there, was not a sufficient reason to depart from what he found to be the clear literal meaning of Descriptor 2c. Note, that although the words supervision, prompting or assistance do not appear in any of the descriptors of this activity, the concept of assistance etc. still applies because the definition of "aided" in art.1 of the Schedule includes all of those terms.

p.909, *amendment to the Employment and Support Allowance Regulations 2008 (SI 2008/794) reg.2(1) (Interpretation—definition of "training allowance")*

With effect from May 26, 2015, Art.2 and Sch.3, para.14(2) of the Deregulation Act 2015 (Consequential Amendments) Order 2015 (SI 2015/971) amended reg.2(1) by omitting the words ", the Chief Executive of Skills Funding".   2.054

pp.931–932, *amendment to the Employment and Support Allowance Regulations 2008 (SI 2008/794) reg.14 (Meaning of education)*

With effect from May 26, 2015, Art.2 and Sch.3, para.14(3) of the Deregulation Act 2015 (Consequential Amendments) Order 2015 (SI 2015/971) amended reg.14(2) by (a) inserting "or section 100 of the Apprenticeships, Skills, Children and Learning Act 2009" after "section 14 of the Education Act 2002" in subpara.(a)(i); (b) omitting subpara.(a)(ia); (c) substituting "or section 100 of the Apprenticeships, Skills, Children and Learning Act 2009" for ", the Chief Executive of Skills Funding" in para.(c); and (d) omitting "under section 14 of the Education Act 2002 or the Chief Executive of Skills Funding"; and (e)   2.055

substituting "the Secretary of State" for "either of those persons" in subpara.(c)(i).

pp.938–942, *annotation to the Employment and Support Allowance Regulations 2008 (SI 2008/794) reg.19(2) and (5) (Determination of limited capability for work)*

2.056   See further on reg.19(5)(b), in the context of activity 15 (getting about), the decision in *MC v SSWP (ESA)* [2015] UKUT 0646 (AAC), discussed in the updating commentary to p.1166 below.

p.963, *annotation to the Employment and Support Allowance Regulations 2008 (SI 2008/794) reg.29(2) (Exceptional circumstances)*

2.057   The extensive passage from Judge Mark's decision in *IJ v SSWP (IB)* [2010] UKUT 408 (AAC) (at para.10) cited in the main volume commentary has been criticised by Judge Lane as being inconsistent with Court of Appeal authority in *Charlton v Secretary of State for Work and Pensions* [2009] EWCA Civ 42; see *MW v SSWP (ESA)* [2015] UKUT 0665 (AAC). The relevant passage in Judge Lane's decision merits citation in full:

> "11. It is noted that the Court of Appeal in *Charlton* thought it possible, *although probably rare*, that the very finding of capability for work might cause a significant deterioration in a claimant's health. Apart from that rarity, the Court of Appeal states firmly that the risk to be assessed must arise *as a consequence of work the claimant would be found capable of undertaking, but for regulation 29.*
>
> 12. In *MB v Secretary of State for Work and Pensions (ESA)* [2012] UKUT 228 (AAC) with which I respectfully agree, Judge Jacobs stated that *Charlton*
>
>> 'decided that the trigger for the risk had to be found in the work the claimant would be undertaking. It had to arise from (i) the decision that the claimant had capability for work; (ii) the work that the claimant might do; or (iii) travelling to and from work. (i) will be rare.
>
>> 13. In *MB* the risk argued before the Tribunal was that if B, a drug addict, had to work, it would put more money in his pocket which he would spend on drugs. Judge Jacobs rejected this argument:
>
>> 'That is not a risk that arises from the work. The work is merely the circumstance that gives rise to it.'
>
>> 14. *Charlton* and *MB v Secretary of State for Work and Pensions* establish that there must be a causal link *between the risk and the work* (or travel to and from work) *the claimant would be found capable of undertaking, but for regulation 29(2)(b).* The Court of Appeal shows that the links in that causal chain are short. There is no hint in *Charlton* that a risk arising from some circumstance short of work, the workplace and getting to and from work, that is to be considered.

15. Tribunals are not dealing with an open-ended inquiry into whether, for example, a claimant who is found not to have limited capability for work would go on to apply for Jobseeker's Allowance, let alone with what would be required of him in his JSA agreement.

16. Policy and practical concerns consistent with the narrow focus under the Social Security (Incapacity for Work) (General) Regulations 1995 and ESA Regulations underpin the Court of Appeal's decision. These are apparent from paragraph [47] of *Charlton;* and although the Court of Appeal's remarks in paragraph 47 are directed at how to establish a range of work that the claimant may do, its remarks are in my view equally applicable to the causation issue.

46 ' . . . Any interpretation must bear in mind that the regulations are designed to provide a fair and effective system for assessing entitlement to incapacity benefit and to allied benefits when a claimant has passed the Personal Capability Assessment. It would not be possible to achieve the aim of those regulations were the decision-maker to be required to make findings of the particularity for which the claimant contends. The decision-maker, it must be recalled, will be provided only with the report of the doctor based upon the doctor's interview with the claimant and the claimant's completion of the questionnaire . . . The conclusion which requires no more than that the decision-maker or Tribunal assess the range of work of which the claimant is capable for the purposes of assessing risk to health has the merit of achieving the objective of the regulations.'

17. Cases in the Upper Tribunal which seek to expand the circumstances in which a claimant might be at risk beyond looking at the work (and travel to and from work) in which the claimant might be engaged but for regulation 29(2)(b) (or beyond the rare exception where the decision itself would cause a substantial risk to health) widen the causational scope of the enquiry in a way that is inconsistent with *Charlton* and should not be followed.

18. It is also unnecessary for Tribunals to follow the remarks in *GS* and *IJ* because they are *obiter.* In *IJ,* Upper Tribunal Judge Mark identified the underlying, fundamental error of the F-tT to be its failure to make the necessary findings of fact on the range of work to which the claimant was suited so that there could be no decision on the work he could do without substantial risk. Judge Mark relied on a standard reformulation of the requirements of *Charlton* in coming to this conclusion.

"9. There was, however, no investigation by the tribunal about the claimant's background to form a view on the range or types of work for which he was both suited as a matter of training or aptitude and which his disabilities did not render him incapable of performing. As a result there was no decision as to whether within that range there was work he could do without the degree of risk to health envisaged by regulation 27(b). In making that assessment the tribunal would have to take into account both the risk to the claimant as a result of his mental health problems and also the limits on the work he could do because of them, including any alcohol dependency he was found to have.

19. This was a more than sufficient basis on which to dispose of the case.

20. In my view, the second part of paragraph 17 of *GS* and paragraph 10 of *IJ* do exactly what the Court was at pains to avoid by diverting 'the proper focus of this issue by an elaboration of the provisions in relation to Jobseeker's Allowance.' The provision of JSA define not only the minimum requirements as to the type of work which the claimant must be available for, but also the number and nature of steps the claimant is required to take to remain entitled to JSA. It is fundamental to the reasoning in *Charlton* that the contents of a hypothetical JSA Agreement did *not* colour the essential feature of regulation 29(2)(b). It was necessary to moor the regulation to its bearing of substantial risk connected to work, the workplace, getting to or from it, or (rarely) being told ESA would end.

21. There are any number of places in *Charlton* at which the Court of Appeal could have indicated that it intended decision makers to take into consideration the wide range of circumstances set out in *IJ and GS*. It would have been very easy for the Court to have added acknowledge the effect of traumas such as getting out of bed in the mornings, travelling to attend interviews fruitlessly, and withstanding adverse economic conditions as relevant, but it did not do so. Its insistence throughout is (apart from the one rare exception envisaged by the Court) on relevant risks connected with travelling to and from work and being at work."

pp.965–966, *annotation to the Employment and Support Allowance Regulations 2008 (SI 2008/794) reg. 29(2) (Exceptional circumstances)*

2.058   The extensive passage from Judge Mark's decision in *GS v SSWP (IB)* [2014] UKUT 16 (AAC) (at paras 16 and 17) cited in the main volume commentary has been criticised by Judge Lane as being inconsistent with Court of Appeal authority in *Charlton v Secretary of State for Work and Pensions* [2009] EWCA Civ 42; see *MW v SSWP (ESA)* [2015] UKUT 0665 (AAC) and see further note to p.963 above.

p.969, *annotation to the Employment and Support Allowance Regulations 2008 (SI 2008/794) reg. 29(2) (Exceptional circumstances)*

2.059   For a further example of a case in which the Upper Tribunal followed the same reasoning as in *NS v Secretary of State for Work and Pensions (ESA)* [2014] UKUT 0115 (AAC), namely that the more obvious it is that reg.29 does not apply, the easier it is to say why that is so, see *JH(S) v Secretary of State for Work and Pensions (ESA)* [2015] UKUT 0567 (AAC). The following observation was made by Judge Hemingway in *RK v Secretary of State for Work and Pensions (ESA)* [2015] UKUT 0549 (AAC), allowing an appeal on the reg.29 point:

"16. I would just wish to add one brief final comment. It seems to me that a consideration of the type or range of work a claimant might reasonably be expected to undertake is something which is often (though by no means always) missed by a tribunal. Often that will not be fatal. Indeed, as was made clear in *NS*, cited above, it will sometimes not be fatal even if regulation 29 is not referred to at all. However, there will be cases, as here, and it seems to me they are not infrequent, where there are indications that the range might be limited for various reasons, perhaps a lack of experience of or aptitude for certain categories of work, perhaps a difficulty with written or spoken English, perhaps an established physical or mental disablement, perhaps something else, such that a proper consideration of this aspect is needed. Of course, the test does not require anything like the sort of detailed analysis which might be involved in, say, testing the degree of risk to health by reference to specific jobs or job descriptions. A short assessment, perhaps only a couple of sentences or so, will often be enough. A tribunal will often already have some background information in the documents before it and will be able to ask questions about the sorts of matters referred to above if an oral hearing is held. Where competent representatives are involved it may well assist a tribunal if any written submission lodged in advance of a hearing can specify whether and on what basis regulation 29 is relied upon and can deal with, if thought to be relevant, the question of the range or type of work."

pp.981–982, *annotation to the Employment and Support Allowance Regulations 2008 (SI 2008/794) reg.34(6) (Determination of limited capability for work-related activity)*

See further the decision of Judge Jacobs in *IC v SSWP (ESA)* [2015] UKUT 0615 (AAC), discussed in the updating note to the commentary on Sch.3 below (note to p.1182).   2.060

pp.986–987, *annotation to the Employment and Support Allowance Regulations 2008 (SI 2008/794) reg.35(2) (Certain claimants to be treated as having limited capability for work-related activity)—But what if the Secretary of State fails to provide the required evidence?*

The decision of the three-judge panel in *IM v SSWP (ESA)* [2014] UKUT 412 (AAC), to be reported as [2015] AACR 10, highlighted "that, because the results of work capability assessments are not routinely passed to providers who determine what work-related activity a claimant should be required to do, there may a risk of a provider requiring a person with, say, mental health problems to perform unsuitable work-related activity, due to the provider's ignorance of the those problems or their extent. This difficulty is liable to be exacerbated if, as in both *IM* and the present case, the claimant is, or is likely to be, unable to engage in social contact with the provider and so explain her difficulties herself" (see *GB v SSWP (ESA)* [2015] UKUT 0200 (AAC), *per* Judge Rowland). This point was further emphasised by Judge Gray in   2.061

XT v SSWP (ESA) [2015] UKUT 0581 (AAC). There the FTT had decided that the appellant could undertake all likely work-related activities with the exception of work placements and work experience (because of her fragile mental health). The FTT found she did not qualify for the support group, working on the assumption that its reservations would be communicated to the relevant provider of work-related activity. That assumption was misplaced in the light of *IM v SSWP (ESA)*. Judge Gray accordingly held the FTT's decision to be in error of law; she went ahead to re-make the decision in the appellant's favour, explaining why there was a substantial risk within the terms of reg.35(2).

p.989, *annotation to the Employment and Support Allowance Regulations 2008 (SI 2008/794) reg.35(2) (Certain claimants to be treated as having limited capability for work-related activity)—Issue 4*

2.062   In *NN-K v Secretary of State for Work and Pensions (ESA)* [2015] UKUT 0385 (AAC) Judge Jacobs reminded tribunals that as a result of the decision in *IM v Secretary of State for Work and Pensions* [2014] UKUT 412 (AAC), to be reported as [2015] AACR 10, a tribunal applying reg.35 must have regard to the type of work-related activity that the claimant might be expected to undertake in her area; in doing so, the tribunal must consider whether the activity would "be reasonable . . . having regard to the person's circumstances" (reg.3(4)(a)). In that context the compatibility of any such activity with a claimant's existing education course would be one of those circumstances (para.9). However:

> "10. But such factors are only relevant in so far as they relate to the existence of a substantial risk to health. The tribunal should ignore any factor that is not relevant to that. If the tribunal does not have, and is not to be treated as having, limited capability for work-related activity, any issues such as the reasonableness of the activity would arise subsequently. In particular, the issue might arise whether to give a direction on work-related activity or whether she had good cause for not undertaking it or whether to reduce her benefit for failing to comply with the direction."

p.990, *annotation to the Employment and Support Allowance Regulations 2008 (SI 2008/794) reg.35(2) (Certain claimants to be treated as having limited capability for work-related activity)—Issue 5*

2.063   *Issue 5: how does reg.35(2) operate if the claimant lives outside the UK?* In *BB v Secretary of State for Work and Pensions (ESA)* [2015] UKUT 0545 (AAC) the claimant lived in Spain and later in the Republic of Ireland. Following a conversion decision he was found to qualify for ESA without the support component. A tribunal dismissed his appeal, finding that reg.35(2) was not satisfied. On appeal to the Upper Tribunal, the Secretary of State's representative confirmed that there were no arrangements in place to provide work-related activities in countries outside the UK and argued that the reg.35(2) test has to be applied on a hypothetical basis, namely "what could happen if a claimant were required to undertake work-related activity, not what would happen" (para.14(b)). Judge Mitchell allowed the claimant's appeal, as he had not had "a fair opportunity to put forward a case in relation to regulation 35(2) because he was unaware of the type of work-related activity by reference to which regulation 35(2) would be applied" (para.20). The Secretary of State's representative further argued that "Where the claimant lives outside the UK and elects to have a paper hearing (as in this case) the hearing is almost always going to take place in Newcastle. However if the claimant chooses to attend in person they can choose a venue suitable to them. Thus, in such cases the relevant WRA evidence will be from the Newcastle area, or the area in which the tribunal was that the claimant attended" (para.17). Remitting the appeal to a new tribunal, Judge Mitchell observed as follows:

"22. I acknowledge the conceptual difficulties raised by the application of regulation 35(2), given the existing authorities, in foreign cases such as this. The Secretary of State's proposed solution has the benefit of levelling, to an extent, the playing field. It reduces the chances of different reg. 35(2) outcomes solely by reason of a person's country of residence. If an appellant does not object, the First-tier Tribunal ought to adopt the course suggested by the Secretary of State. If the appellant does object, the Tribunal will need to decide for itself how to proceed taking into account the reasons for the objection and any submissions of the Secretary of State" (para.22).

p.1082, *amendment to the Employment and Support Allowance Regulations 2008 (SI 2008/794) reg.131 (Interpretation)*

2.064   With effect from May 26, 2015, art.2 and Sch.3, para.14(4)(a) of the Deregulation Act 2015 (Consequential Amendments) Order 2015 (SI 2015/971) amended the definition of "access funds" by omitting "the Chief Executive of Skills Funding" from para.(d).

pp.1083–1084, *amendment to the Employment and Support Allowance Regulations 2008 (SI 2008/794) reg.131 (Interpretation)*

2.065   With effect from May 26, 2015, art.2 and Sch.3, para.14(4)(b) of the Deregulation Act 2015 (Consequential Amendments) Order 2015 (SI 2015/971) amended the definition of "full-time course of advanced education" by (a) substituting "or under section 100 of the Apprenticeships, Skills, Children and Learning Act 2009" for ", the Chief Executive of Skills Funding" in para.(a); (b) substituting "or under section 100 of the Apprenticeships, Skills, Children and Learning Act 2009" for ", the Chief Executive of Skills Funding" in para.(b); and (c) omitting "under section 14 of the Education Act 2002 or the Chief Executive of Skills Funding" and substituting "the Secretary of State" for "either of those persons" in para.(b)(i).

pp.1084–1085, *amendment to the Employment and Support Allowance Regulations 2008 (SI 2008/794) reg.131 (Interpretation)*

2.066   With effect from May 26, 2015, art.2 and Sch.3, para.14(4)(c) of the Deregulation Act 2015 (Consequential Amendments) Order 2015 (SI 2015/971) amended the definition of "full-time course of study" by (i) substituting "or section 100 of the Apprenticeships, Skills, Children and Learning Act 2009" for ", the Chief Executive of Skills Funding" in para.(a); substituting "or section 100 of the Apprenticeships, Skills, Children and Learning Act 2009" for ", the Chief Executive of Skills Funding" in para.(b); and (iii) omitting "under section 14 of the Education Act 2002 or the Chief Executive of Skills Funding" and substituting "the Secretary of State" for "either of those persons" in para.(b)(i).

p.1143, *annotation to the Employment and Support Allowance Regulations 2008 (SI 2008/794) Sch.2 (Assessment of whether a claimant has limited capability for work: evidence and attention to detail)*

2.067   On the issue of the duty to provide previous medical reports, a three-judge panel in *FN v SSWP (ESA)* [2015] UKUT 670 (AAC) (formerly CSE/422/2013, CSE/435/2013 and CSE/19/2014) has broadly agreed with decisions such as *JC v DSD (IB)* [2011] NICom 177; [2014] AACR 30 and also both *ST v SSWP (ESA)* [2012] UKUT 469 (AAC) and *AM v SSWP (ESA)* [2013] UKUT 458 (AAC). The three-judge panel stressed that the previous adjudication history and associated evidence is not *always* relevant to an employment and support allowance appeal and that, even if the Secretary of State has not produced all the information and evidence that he should have produced with his response to an appeal, it does not necessarily follow that the First-tier Tribunal's decision will be wrong in law and liable to be set aside.

> "79. . . . We can envisage a situation where a First-tier Tribunal considers that it has sufficient relevant evidence before it to determine the issues arising in the appeal without the requirement to call for evidence which is missing because the Secretary of State has failed in his duty to provide it.
> 80. . . . Our view is that the first choice for the tribunal should not be to adjourn but to get on with the task of determining the issues arising in the appeal when satisfied that it has the necessary relevant evidence before it. It might be the case that having weighed and assessed the appellant's oral evidence, the tribunal might be satisfied that the evidence is credible, should be accepted and the appeal be allowed. . . . "

See further the updating commentary to pp.629 and 1605 of Vol.III (below).

p.1152, *annotation to the Employment and Support Allowance Regulations 2008 (SI 2008/794) Sch.2 Activity 1: Mobilising unaided*

2.068   A claimant's ability to mobilise *with* significant discomfort or exhaustion should be disregarded for the purposes of Activity 1: see *GL v*

Secretary of State for Work and Pensions (ESA) [2015] UKUT 0503 (AAC).

p.1153, *annotation to the Employment and Support Allowance Regulations 2008 (SI 2008/794) Sch.2 Activity 2: Standing and sitting*

The decision of Judge Ward in *EC v SSWP (ESA)* [2015] UKUT   **2.069**
0618 (AAC) considers the conflict in the case law on the pre-March 2011 version of the Activity 2 descriptors. Those cases included *MC v SSWP* [2012] UKUT 324 (AAC); [2013] AACR 13 (Judge Wikeley) and *EW v SSWP (ESA)* [2013] UKUT 0228 (AAC) (Judge Williams), both holding that an inability remain at a work station by one route alone (standing or sitting) was not enough for a claimant to qualify for points. However, in *MM v Department for Social Development (ESA)* [2014] NICom 48 (Northern Ireland Tribunal of three Commissioners) and *MT v Department for Social Development* (ESA) NICom 53 (Commissioner Stockman) disagreed on the issue of the relevance of a person's ability to achieve the requisite period through combining standing and sitting.

Judge Ward in *EC v SSWP (ESA)* held that there were "compelling reasons" to depart from the decision of the Tribunal of Commissioners in *MM v Department for Social Development (ESA)*. In doing so, he analysed a range of materials which shed light on the issues relevant to the interpretation of the Activity 2 descriptors:

> "57. In conclusion, it seems to me that an argument based on informed interpretation, if relying on a committee report, needs to be based on its final form and to take into account other material which Parliament must be taken as having had in mind when approving the legislation. In the light of the totality of the material before me, I accept that the mischief at which the legislation was aimed, on this aspect, included ensuring that people who could remain at a work-station for the requisite period by combining sitting and standing would not get points. Seen against that background, the ambiguity in the use of the "either . . . or" construction in the descriptors in activity 2 between 2011 and 2013 would fall to be resolved in accordance with Judge Wikeley's obiter views in *MT.* The Tribunal of Commissioners in *MM* did not have the advantage that I have now had, through oral submissions and subsequent written submissions, of comprehensive examination of the background materials leading up to the making of the Regulations. In those circumstances, while I have applied a test of whether there is a "compelling reason" to depart from the decision in *MM*, I have concluded that there is. With the benefit of those fuller submissions (which it appears were not made in *MC* or *MT* either) I conclude that a person who can remain at a workstation by a combination of sitting and standing for the requisite period is not entitled to points."

A separate point in relation to Activity 2 was considered by Judge   **2.070**
Mitchell in *LC v SSWP (ESA)* [2015] UKUT 0664 (AAC), namely what is meant by "at a workstation" in descriptors 2b and 2c. The judge

held that the First-tier Tribunal had erred in law by failing to address whether the claimant could fairly be said to have been capable of performing a job of work while remaining sat "at a workstation" in the light of her evidence that she needed to sit with one leg stretched rigidly out in front of her. Judge Mitchell concluded as follows:

> "23. I conclude, therefore, that when descriptors 2(b) and 2(c) refer to a person remaining "at a workstation" they refer to the person being orientated towards a workstation, whether sitting or standing, in such a manner that they may fairly be described as capable of performing a job of work. I do not think I need to go any further than this in interpreting the descriptor by, for example, attempting to define a workstation. I can leave it to the good sense of tribunals, using their knowledge of everyday life and their specialist expertise, to apply that test.
>
> 24. If, therefore, a person needs to sit with a rigidly outstretched leg so that s/he could not fairly be said to be capable of doing a job of work at a workstation, even with the benefits supplied by an adjustable chair, this would not amount to the person remaining sat "at a work station".
>
> 25. So far as section 20 of the Equality Act 2010 (reasonable adjustments) is concerned, I see no need for tribunals to try and predict how it might operate in a particular case. Attempting to identify the content of any particular reasonable adjustment divorced from a real world case is very difficult and liable to introduce unnecessary confusion and complexity. The question of what is reasonable is informed by two sets of variables: the characteristics of the disabled person and the entity obliged to make the adjustment. What might be reasonable for a small independent trader could well differ from what is required of a well-resourced multinational corporation. Instead, tribunals should simply rely on their own knowledge and expertise in applying the descriptors by envisaging the typical workstations and adjustable chairs with which I suspect we are all familiar."

pp.1155–1157, *annotation to the Employment and Support Allowance Regulations 2008 (SI 2008/794) Sch.2 Activity 6: Manual dexterity*

2.071 In *SM v SSWP (ESA)* [2015] UKUT 0617 (AAC) the appellant had been with congenital deformities to both hands, involving the fusion of certain fingers. One of the issues on the appeal was Descriptor 5c: "cannot use a pen or pencil to make a meaningful mark with either hand". The claimant's appeal was allowed on a reg.29 point. However, Judge Ward expressed the following view:

> "7. It follows that I have received only brief submissions from the parties about descriptor 5 (c). The tribunal found as fact that the claimant could write his signature. It certainly is an issue before me (I am not clear whether it was before the First-tier Tribunal) whether he can do so with reasonable regularity but that is something for the tribunal to which this case is remitted to explore. The claimant's representative draws attention to varies definitions of "meaningful". In

my view descriptor 5(c) is not concerned with marks that are "meaningful" in the sense of "having great meaning, eloquent, expressive" (per Collins dictionary). That is a sense which might be appropriate when "meaningful" is applied to, for instance, glances, but is not a natural sense when applied to something such as rudimentary as a mark with a pen or pencil. Rather, I consider that it in this context means "having meaning" as opposed to "not having meaning". Further than that I prefer not to go in this case."

p.1157, *annotation to the Employment and Support Allowance Regulations 2008 (SI 2008/794) Sch.2 Activity 7: Understanding communication*

The version of Activity 7 in force before January 28, 2013 was ana-   2.072
lysed by Judge Markus QC in *AT and VC v Secretary of State for Work and Pensions (ESA)* [2015] UKUT 0445 (AAC), to be reported as [2016] AACR 8. However, her decision is also relevant to the current formulation of the descriptors (see para.54). At the outset Judge Markus noted that the terms "verbal" and "non-verbal" are confusing "because both forms of understanding in activity 7 relate to verbal communications, in that the activity is about understanding words whether written or spoken" Thus ""verbal" is used to mean "spoken" and "non-verbal" is used to mean "written"" (para.37). Further, the drafting left it ambiguous as to "whether a claimant must be unable to understand or have difficulty in understanding communication by both verbal and non-verbal means in order to satisfy the relevant descriptors, or whether inability/difficulty by only one of those means is sufficient" (para.1).
Judge Markus therefore considered the legislative history of activity 7 and its antecedents. This led her to conclude "that in order to qualify under a relevant descriptor a claimant need be impaired in either hearing or vision (but not both) or, as amended, in understanding either spoken or written communication (but not both)" (para.48). The current formulation "is not much of an improvement on the previous wording" (para.50), but the judge was satisfied "that the word "alone" was inserted after each of (i) and (ii) with the intention of making clear that it is sufficient if a person is unable to understand a message by either verbal or non-verbal means" (para.51).

p.1165, *annotation to the Employment and Support Allowance Regulations 2008 (SI 2008/794) Sch.2 Activity 13: Initiating and completing personal action*

Activity 13 was further considered by Judge Jacobs in *MP v Secretary*   2.073
of State for Work and Pensions (ESA) [2015] UKUT 0458 (AAC), where he noted it was "neither necessary nor appropriate to define 'personal action'. They are ordinary words that have to be given their normal meaning" (see *Moyna v Secretary of State for Work and Pensions* [2003] 1 WLR 1929 at [24]). Accordingly, "At the risk of stating the obvious, it means something undertaken by someone on their own" (para.23). Judge Jacobs held that the tribunal "must apply common sense in

deciding what constitutes an action. It is possible to render the legislation redundant by splitting an action into its component parts. The definition of Activity 13 recognises this by referring to 'tasks' as components of a single action" (para.28). Judge Jacobs provided the following further analysis (Mr Leithead appeared for the claimant, Ms Blackmore for the Secretary of State):

30. I accept Mr Leithead's argument that actions that are undertaken out of habit are not to be considered. Their performance does not demonstrate the claimant's mental, cognitive or intellectual function. They merely show that the claimant has developed the habit of performing them. I accept Mr Leithead's argument that *DK* can be distinguished on the ground that it was concerned specifically to test memory and concentration.

31. I accept Ms Blackmore's argument that the action must be effective. Actions are not undertaken for their own sake. They are undertaken for a reason and a purpose. If that purpose cannot be achieved, the action is ineffective. The activity is defined as initiating *and completing* personal action. If the action never reaches the point of being effective, it is not complete. The most obvious example is a person with obsessive compulsive disorder. A person with that disorder is able to perform particular actions and to do so regularly, reliably and repeatedly. Their difficulty is being unable to stop doing them. The result is that they are unable to continue with the rest of their life. For those without the disorder, the action would be part of their life and allows them to continue with the rest of their life. For those with the disorder, the actions becomes their life and prevents them continuing with the activities they would then wish to pursue.

32. In considering effectiveness, it is important to remember the purpose of the test, which is to decide whether it is reasonable to require the claimant to work.

33. Activity 13 further defines initiating and completing person action as meaning 'planning, organisation, problem solving, prioritising or switching tasks'. I accept Mr Leithead's argument that, in descriptors (a), (b) and (c), 'or' must be read conjunctively, as meaning 'and'. Ms Blackmore agreed with that argument, which reflects the description of the activity itself, which uses 'and'.

34. The tribunal's decision on Activity 13 must relate only to actions that involve all these tasks. This does not mean that the tribunal must find evidence of an action involving all those tasks that the claimant cannot complete. It may be that there will be evidence from, say, dressing that shows the claimant being unable to plan by selecting appropriate clothing to wear outdoors, which can be put together with evidence from, say, cooking, that shows the claimant being unable to prioritise tasks. This specific evidence may have to be supplemented by inferences drawn from the nature of the claimant's condition or other factors.

35. This does not mean that the action considered need necessarily be complicated, so long as the tribunal takes all potential tasks into account. Take dressing as an example. Most of the time dressing may

simply be routine. It may even involve nothing more than putting on the clothing selected and laid out by the claimant's partner. But it can require planning (deciding what to wear), organising (assembling the different items required), problem solving (finding an alternative item of clothing for something that is in the wash), prioritising (deciding whether it is more important to get dressed or to wash a particular item of clothing) or switching tasks (going to iron a shirt to wear). To put it differently. The tribunal must always be sure that the evidence on which it relies actually demonstrates an ability to undertake all the tasks required by the activity.

36. The claimant must not be prejudiced by living a limited life-style. It may be that someone whose daily life is limited to the basic actions of survival and watching the television would have difficulties if required to undertake any action that was more complicated. This is really an instance of the point I have just made about evidence and proof. It is also an instance of Ms Blackmore's argument that actions must be effective to allow a person to function. That is what the activity tests: function, not survival.

37. I trust that it is now clear why, for a variety of reasons, tribunals have been wrong when they have treated cleaning teeth and washing as separate and sequential personal actions.

38. I accept Mr Leithead's argument that there is no test of the severity of the condition. It is nowhere stated in the legislation and it is inconsistent with the provisions that the legislation does contain. The legislation is a test of capability and disability. It is the experience of every judge who has dealt with capability and disablement issues that conditions that would medically be classified as serious or severe do not necessarily generate incapacity or disability, whilst conditions that would medically be classified as mild can generate incapacity and disability. To put it another way, severity is tested not by reference to the medical condition, but by reference to the manner and extent in which it restricts a claimant's activities.

39. This is not to say that the nature of the claimant's medical condition is irrelevant. That condition is relevant to the threshold requirement that the activities in Part 2 of Schedule 2 are only relevant if they arise from 'a specific mental illness or disablement' that affects the claimant's 'mental, cognitive and intellectual function'. The condition may also provide a basis for drawing an inference that the claimant is, or is not, likely to experience particular restrictions. And the nature of the condition provides a check when assessing the evidence on whether the difficulties that the claimant reports are likely to arise from the condition.

40. I accept Ms Blackmore's argument that the amendment adding 'sequential' to descriptors (b) and (c) merely made explicit what consistency had always required. This is comparable to the decision of Judge White in *CS v Secretary of State for Work and Pensions* [2014] UKUT 0519 (AAC) that the words 'on level ground' had to be read into the language of some of the descriptors for Activity 1.

41. I reject Mr Leithead's argument that sequential means that the actions 'should bear close relation to each other so as to form a logical

sequence.' As with so many words, 'sequential' and 'consecutive' can be used interchangeably or they can convey different nuances of meanings. Both convey that the actions must occur separately rather than at the same time. If anything, the former conveys the notion captured by Ms Blackmore that the actions must occur in the same time frame. That is consistent with the actions having to be effective. The concept of effectiveness involves functioning, and being able to perform only a single personal action in a particular time frame is hardly consistent with functioning effectively. I see no reason, though, why the actions should be related one to another, as Mr Leithead argued."

p.1166, *annotation to the Employment and Support Allowance Regulations 2008 (SI 2008/794) Sch.2 Activity 15: Getting about*

2.074   Descriptor 1 of Activity 15 is satisfied if a claimant "cannot get to any place outside the claimant's home with which the claimant is familiar". "Any place outside the claimant's home" means more than simply beyond their front door. According to Judge Bano in *PC v Secretary of State for Work and Pensions (ESA)* [2015] UKUT 0531 (AAC), "For my part, I do not consider that putting out the bins or going outside to have a cigarette amounts to 'getting about', even if there is a chance of meeting a neighbour or visitor to the building when doing so. In my judgment, descriptor 1 of Activity 15 requires an investigation of whether a claimant can go to a place outside the immediate vicinity of their home, and that in order to satisfy the descriptor it is not necessary for a claimant to establish that he or she cannot go beyond their front door" (para.8).

Activity 15 was also in issue in *MC v SSWP (ESA)* [2015] UKUT 0646 (AAC). According to Judge Rowland,

> "the correct approach, best giving effect to the purpose behind the legislation—is that the claimant's "specific mental illness or disablement" had to be an *effective* cause of her inability to go out unaccompanied. That is not the same as being the root cause or the primary cause. In my judgement, where a specific mental illness or disablement would not by itself have been sufficiently serious to enable a claimant to satisfy a descriptor, it is enough for the purposes of regulation 19(5)(b) that it has made the difference between the claimant being able to satisfy a descriptor and not being able to do so even though there may have been another, perhaps more important, cause" (at para.9).

p.1180, *annotation to the Employment and Support Allowance Regulations 2008 (SI 2008/794) Sch.3 Activity 7: Understanding communication*

2.075   Judge Markus QC in *AT and VC v SSWP (ESA)* [2015] UKUT 0445 (AAC) was "satisfied that activity 7 in Schedule 3 was intended to correspond with the highest descriptor in activity 7 of Schedule 2" (para.53). Furthermore, as with Sch.2, Activity 7 (both in its current and previous formulations: see para 54) "applied to a claimant who was unable to communicate by either verbal means or non-verbal means and it was not necessary for the claimant to be unable to communicate by both means" (para.53).

p.1182, *annotation to the Employment and Support Allowance Regulations 2008 (SI 2008/794) Sch.3 Activity 16: Chewing or swallowing food or drink*

Judge Wikeley's decision in *WC v SSWP (ESA)* [2015] UKUT 304 (AAC), to be reported as [2016] AACR 1, was considered by Judge Jacobs in *IC v SSWP (ESA)* [2015] UKUT 0615 (AAC), where the specific question that arose was whether a claimant can satisfy either descriptor 16a or 16b on account of the difficulties he experiences as a result of his false teeth. Judge Jacobs held that there was simply no evidence that activity 16 could apply on the facts of the instant case, given the requirements of reg.34(6)(b); thus there was no evidence that the claimant's difficulties with his false teeth arose from a specific bodily disease or disablement or from treatment (para.13). Judge Jacobs continued, without deciding, to consider whether false teeth are and aid or appliance (within reg.34(3)(b)) or a prosthesis (within reg.35(3)(a)) (para.14). Judge Jacobs stressed further the importance of applying the statutory test, rather than a substitute test, and gave the following guidance: 2.076

> "16. This brings me to another way to frame the issue, which is to concentrate on the food rather than the chewing. As I put it in my preliminary observations: what sort of food is envisaged by the descriptor? Again, there is a range of possibilities. It is not necessary to be able to eat any food, from the most tender to the toughest. That would set too demanding a standard. But liquidised food is a liquid, more akin to a drink than food, and does not require chewing.
>
> 17. A third, and better, way to frame the issue is to take the whole expression and ask: what is involved in chewing food? That at least preserves the immediate context. It makes the expression as a whole the object of the enquiry, rather than its individual components. It does not, though, produce any clear answer.
>
> 18. On any formulation, it is important to remember the context, which is a test of whether a claimant's capability for work and for work-related activity is restricted sufficiently to qualify for an employment and support allowance. The disability need not have a direct effect on the performance of work or work-related activity, as feeding oneself is not going to be involved in either case. So the scope of the Activity cannot be calibrated by its effect in those contexts. Nevertheless the effect of satisfying a descriptor in terms of benefit entitlement indicates that the disability should be significant. It must be such that 'it is not reasonable to require' the claimant to undertake work or the activity, to use the language of section 8(1) and 9(1) of the Welfare Reform Act 2007. The passage in the WCA Handbook reflects that, although it is not presented (and must not be taken) as a comprehensive statement of the physical conditions that can lead to the disabilities in Activity 16(a) and (b)."

pp.1185–1186, *amendment to the Employment and Support Allowance Regulations 2008 (SI 2008/794) Sch.4 (Amounts) para.6 (Severe disability premium)*

2.077 With effect from November 4, 2015, reg.19 of the Universal Credit and Miscellaneous Amendments Regulations 2015 (SI 2015/1754) amended para.6 to read as follows:

Severe disability premium

6.—(1) The condition is that the claimant is a severely disabled person.

(2) For the purposes of sub-paragraph (1), a claimant is to be treated as being a severely disabled person if, and only if—

(a) in the case of a single claimant, a lone parent, a person who has no partner and who is responsible for and a member of the same household as a young person or a claimant who is treated as having no partner in consequence of sub-paragraph (3)—

(i) the claimant is in receipt of the care component, the daily living component, armed forces independence payment or attendance allowance;

(ii) subject to sub-paragraph (4), the claimant has no non-dependants aged 18 or over normally residing with the claimant or with whom the claimant is normally residing; and

(iii) no person is entitled to, and in receipt of, a carer's allowance under section 70 of the Contributions and Benefits Act [a carer's allowance or has an award of universal credit which includes the carer element] in respect of caring for the claimant;

(b) in the case of a claimant who has a partner—

(i) the claimant is in receipt of the care component, the daily living component, armed forces independence payment or attendance allowance;

(ii) the claimant's partner is also in receipt of the care component, the daily living component, armed forces independence payment or attendance allowance or, if the claimant is a member of a polygamous marriage, all the partners of that marriage are in receipt of the care component, the daily living component, armed forces independence payment or attendance allowance; and

(iii) subject to sub-paragraph (4), the claimant has no non-dependants aged 18 or over normally residing with the claimant or with whom the claimant is normally residing,

and, either a person is entitled to, and in receipt of, a carer's allowance [or has an award of universal credit which includes the carer element] in respect of caring for only one of the couple or, in the case of a polygamous marriage, for one or more but not all the partners of the marriage or, as the case may be, no person is entitled to, and in receipt of, such an allowance [or has such an award of universal credit] in respect of caring for either member of the couple or any partner of the polygamous marriage.

(3) Where a claimant has a partner who does not satisfy the condition in sub-paragraph (2) (b)(ii) and that partner is blind or severely sight impaired or is treated as blind or severely sight impaired that partner is to be treated for the purposes of sub-paragraph (2) as if the partner were not a partner of the claimant.

(4) For the purposes of sub-paragraph (2)(a)(ii) and (b)(iii) no account is to be taken of—

(a) a person receiving attendance allowance, the daily living component, armed forces independence payment or the care component;

(b) subject to sub-paragraph (7), a person who joins the claimant's household for the first time in order to care for the claimant or the claimant's partner and immediately before so joining the claimant or the claimant's partner was treated as a severely disabled person; or

(c) a person who is blind or severely sight impaired or is treated as blind or severely sight impaired.

(5) For the purposes of sub-paragraph (2)(b) a person is to be treated—

(a) as being in receipt of attendance allowance or the care component if the person would, but for the person being a patient for a period exceeding 28 days, be so in receipt;

(b) as being entitled to, and in receipt of, a carer's allowance [or having an award of universal credit which includes the carer element] if the person would, but for the person for whom the person was caring being a patient in hospital for a period exceeding 28 days, be so entitled and in receipt [of carer's allowance or have such an award of universal credit].

(c) as being in entitled to, and in receipt of, the daily living component if the person would, but for regulations under section 86(1) (hospital in-patients) of the 2012 Act, be so entitled and in receiPt

(6) For the purposes of sub-paragraph (2)(a)(iii) and (b), no account is to be taken of an award of carer's allowance [or universal credit which includes the carer element] to the extent that payment of such an award is backdated for a period before the date on which the award is first paid.

(7) Sub-paragraph (4)(b) is to apply only for the first 12 weeks following the date on which the person to whom that provision applies first joins the claimant's household.

(8) In sub-paragraph (2)(a)(iii) and (b), references to a person being in receipt of a carer's allowance [or as having an award of universal credit which includes the carer element] are to include references to a person who would have been in receipt of that allowance [or had such an award] but for the application of a restriction under section 6B or 7 of the Social Security Fraud Act 2001 (loss of benefit provisions).

(9) [(a)] In this paragraph—

"blind or severely sight impaired" means certified as blind or severely sight impaired by a consultant ophthalmologist and a person who has ceased to be certified as blind or severely sight impaired where that person's eyesight has been regained is, nevertheless, to be treated as blind or severely sight impaired for a period of 28 weeks following the date on which the person ceased to be so certified;

"the care component" means the care component of disability living allowance at the highest or middle rate prescribed in accordance with section 72(3) of the Contributions and Benefits Act.

[(b) A person has an award of universal credit which includes the carer element if the person has an award of universal credit which includes an amount which is the carer element under regulation 29 of the Universal Credit Regulations 2013.]

p.1536, *amendment to the Employment and Support Allowance Regulations 2013 (SI 2013/379) reg.2 (Interpretation)*

2.078   With effect from May 26, 2015, art.2 and Sch.3, para.26 of the Deregulation Act 2015 (Consequential Amendments) Order 2015 (SI 2015/971) amended the definition of "training allowance" by omitting ", the Chief Executive of Skills Funding" in para.(a).

PART III

UPDATING MATERIAL
VOLUME II

INCOME SUPPORT, JOBSEEKER'S ALLOWANCE, STATE PENSION CREDIT AND THE SOCIAL FUND

Commentary by

Penny Wood

Richard Poynter

Nick Wikeley

John Mesher

p.xix, *Using this Book—Northern Ireland legislation*

As mentioned in the main volume, the Welfare Reform and Work Bill that was intended to replicate in Northern Ireland most of the provisions of the Welfare Reform Act 2012 failed to pass its final stage in the Northern Ireland Assembly in May 2015 because it had not gained the necessary cross-community support. This had substantial budgetary implications because the United Kingdom Government funds welfare in Northern Ireland only up to the levels that apply in Great Britain and the 2012 Act had achieved a substantial reduction of expenditure in Great Britain. In consequence, there were 11 weeks of talks between the United Kingdom Government, Northern Ireland politicians and the Irish Government (under the approach required by the 1998 Belfast Agreement), leading to an agreement on November 17, 2015 which resulted in the Northern Ireland (Welfare Reform) Act 2015 being passed by the United Kingdom Parliament and receiving Royal Assent on November 25, 2015. It is a short statute, authorising the making of Orders in Council to make provision in connection with social security in Northern Ireland, provided that any such Order in Council is made by the end of 2016. The Welfare Reform (Northern Ireland) Order 2015 (SI 2015/2006) was duly made on December 9, 2015 and, by virtue of s.2 of the Act, is treated as an Act of the Northern Ireland Assembly. It is similar to the Bill that had failed in the Assembly seven months earlier. Most of the provisions in it will come into force in accordance with commencement orders made by the Department for Social Development. Northern Ireland legislation will then converge again with Great Britain legislation and, for instance, personal independence payment will be introduced in Northern Ireland.

p.34, *annotation to s.1(2) of the old style Jobseekers Act 1995 (Conditions of entitlement)*

In para.(2) of the note (has entered into a jobseeker's agreement, which remains in force), substitute "Jobcentre" for "Jobcenter". See the entry for p.76 on when an agreement remains in force.   3.001

p.61, *annotation to s.6(1) of the old style Jobseekers Act 1995 (Availability: meaning of "any employed earner's employment")*

The reasoning in *GP v SSWP (JSA)* [2015] UKUT 373 (AAC) (see entry for p.68) would indicate that only availability for employment in Great Britain is in issue.   3.002

p.66, *annotation to s.7(1) of the old style Jobseekers Act 1995 (Actively seeking employment)*

If, in relation to the question of whether the steps taken by a claimant give the best prospects of securing employment, the Secretary of State   3.003

asserts to a First-tier Tribunal that there were suitable roles on the Universal Job Match website that the claimant could have applied for, but had not, evidence of such availability to validate the assertion should be produced (para.11 of *RD v SSWP (JSA)* [2015] UKUT 702 (AAC)).

p.68, *annotation to s.7(8) of the old style Jobseekers Act 1995 (Actively seeking employment: definition of "employed earner's employment")*

3.004   In *GP v SSWP (JSA)* [2015] UKUT 373 (AAC), it was held that the incorporation of the terms of the definition of "employed earner's employment" in s.2(1)(a) of the SSCBA 1992 means that steps directed to securing employment that is not in Great Britain cannot count for the purpose of satisfying the test in s.7(1). In the particular case, the claimant was a highly qualified research scientist who, having been unsuccessful in seeking work in the United Kingdom in her field or in more menial jobs, was looking only for jobs in China and had in the period in question arranged two interviews there. Judge Gray decided that the claimant's entitlement to JSA was rightly terminated. She mentioned the oddity that the s.2(1) definition is restricted to Great Britain, rather than the United Kingdom. That would on its face exclude from entitlement claimants taking steps only to secure employment in Northern Ireland. If that conclusion cannot be right, could it be argued that, despite the specific terms of s.7(8), the restriction to employment in Great Britain should be ignored? There is no similar restriction in relation to the work search requirement in new style JSA.

pp.72–73, *annotation to s.9 of the old style Jobseekers Act 1995 (Jobseeker's agreement)*

3.005   In relation to the proper contents of a jobseeker's agreement and the prescribed requirements in subs.(1) and reg.31 of the JSA Regulations 1996, the decision in *PT v SSWP (JSA)* [2015] UKUT 703 (AAC) (not in itself of any citable authority as given with the consent of both parties) records an interesting proposition put forward by the Secretary of State. It was accepted that the proper purpose of the agreement is to set out the details of the claimant's jobseeking, not to include "sanctionable activities". Thus, a requirement to attend "skills conditionality for [Universal Jobmatch]/CV workshop" should not have been proposed to become part of a varied jobseeker's agreement. It was accepted that any condition of opening a Universal Jobmatch account should be imposed through a direction under s.19A(2)(c) of the old style Jobseekers Act 1995. Any requirement to attend a Skills Conditionality Scheme should be imposed through reg.3(7) of the Jobseeker's Allowance (SAPOE) Regulations 2013 (p.1375 of the main volume).

   CH v SSWP (JSA) [2015] UKUT 373 (AAC), mentioned briefly on p.72 of the main volume, discusses the nature of the proper procedure under s.9(6) and (7) when a claimant is not prepared to accept an initial jobseeker's agreement in the terms proposed by the employment officer.

It also criticises some of the administrative guidance in operation at the dates in question there. If there is a reference to the Secretary of State, either at the claimant's request or under the employment officer's discretion, the decision on the reference cannot go beyond determining the questions under s.9(6) and directions under s.9(7). In *CH*, it appeared that the decision given by the Secretary of State did not deal with those questions, but went straight to a decision that the claimant was not entitled to JSA because he had not entered into a jobseeker's agreement. That decision had to be set aside for the reference procedure to be followed. Judge Ward noted in para.39 that the Secretary of State accepted that any physical or mental limitations on a claimant's jobseeking ability should be considered under s.9(6). Also note the possibility of claiming a hardship payment under Sch.1, paras 8 and 10, and JSA Regulations 1996, regs 140-146H while a jobseeker's agreement has not been entered into.

An appeal currently before the Upper Tribunal (*CJSA/1116/2015* and *1118/2015*) raises the issue of whether the form of "claimant commitment" (i.e. in law a jobseeker's agreement) in use from 2014 onwards is affected by the same defect as identified in *CH* in relation to the earlier form (see the main volume).

p.76, *annotation to s.10 of the old style Jobseekers Act 1995 (Variation of jobseeker's agreement)*

In *HS v SSWP (JSA)* [2015] UKUT 701 (AAC), the claimant   3.006
refused to sign a new jobseeker's agreement (under the title of a claimant commitment), not being satisfied with its terms (on the basis accepted by Judge Turnbull). The employment officer referred the matter to the Secretary of State, who gave a decision that the claimant was not entitled to JSA because he had not entered into a jobseeker's agreement. As agreed by the Secretary of State before the Upper Tribunal, the claimant's refusal to sign the new agreement did not entitle the making of a decision to terminate entitlement. Under s.10(5) and (6)(b) the Secretary of State could only decide whether the proposed agreement was compatible with the requirements of availability for employment and actively seeking employment and whether it was reasonable to expect the claimant to comply with the proposed terms and give directions about whether the agreement should be varied and the terms on which it was to be entered into. The existing jobseeker's agreement could not be brought to an end under s.10(6)(c) (so ending satisfaction of the condition of entitlement in s.1(2)(b)) until the expiry of the period of 21 days for the claimant to sign the varied agreement.

p.97, *annotation to s.19 of the old style Jobseekers Act 1995 (Higher-level sanction)*

See the entry for p.199 for references to literature on sanctions pol-   3.007
icy.

p.113, *annotation to s.19(2)(e) of the old style Jobseekers Act 1995 (sanction for failing to participate in a scheme prescribed under s.17A(1))*

3.007.1   See the entry for p.117 below for authority arguably relevant to the issue of good reason under this provision.

p.116, *annotation to s.19A(c) of the old style Jobseekers Act 1995 (Sanction for refusal or failure to comply with a jobseeker's direction)*

3.008   In *SA v SSWP (JSA)* [2015] UKUT 454 the claimant, who had hearing difficulties and wore a hearing aid in one ear, was directed by an employment officer to attend and complete a CV writing course with Learn Direct two days later from 11.15 a.m. to 12.15 p.m. He was given a letter to confirm the time and date. The claimant arrived at 11.25 a.m. and was told that he was too late and so had been deemed to have missed his appointment. He immediately went to the Jobcentre Plus office to rebook an appointment for the course and explained that he had mis-heard the time for the appointment as 11.50, the time that he normally signed on. A fixed four-week sanction for failing, without a good reason, to carry out a reasonable jobseeker's direction was imposed. On appeal the claimant said that at the meeting with the employment officer he had not been wearing his hearing aid and that he had not thought to check the time of the appointment on the letter as he genuinely thought that it was the same as his two previous appointments. The First-tier Tribunal regarded it as clear that the direction had been reasonable and that the claimant had failed to comply with it, so that the sole question was whether he had had a good reason for the failure. On that question, although accepting that the claimant had made a genuine error, the tribunal concluded that that did not in itself give him a good reason and that he had failed to take reasonable steps to confirm the time of the appointment and dismissed his appeal. In setting aside the tribunal's decision and substituting her own decision reversing the imposition of the sanction (as had been suggested by the Secretary of State), Judge Knowles QC held that the tribunal had erred in law by failing to consider the question of whether the claimant had failed to comply with the direction. In the substituted decision, she concluded that, the claimant not having refused to carry out the direction and taking into account that his error was genuine and that he took immediate steps to rebook, it was disproportionate to treat his late arrival in isolation as amounting to a failure to comply with the direction. That can only be regarded as a determination on the particular facts that does not constitute any sort of precedent to be applied as a matter of law in other cases. The outcome may have reflected an understandable desire in a deserving case to get around the absence of any scope for varying the fixed period of four weeks for a s.19A sanction for a "first offence". However, there could have been nothing unreasonable about a conclusion that arriving 10 minutes after the beginning of a course that only lasted for an hour amounted to a failure to comply with a direction to attend and complete the course, no matter how genuine the error that led to the late arrival.

In discussing whether the tribunal had also approached the question of good reason properly, Judge Knowles accepted the Secretary of State's submission that all the circumstances should be considered and that the question was whether those circumstances would have caused a reasonable person to act as the claimant did, provided that the reasonable person was given the characteristics of the claimant in question.

p.117, *annotation to s.19A(2)(d)–(f) of the old style Jobseekers Act 1995 (sanctions for neglecting to avail oneself of a reasonable opportunity of a place on a training scheme or employment programme, failing to apply for or accept if offered a place on such a scheme or programme or giving up a place or failing to attend such a scheme or programme)*

In *PL v DSD (JSA)* [2015] NI Com 72, the Chief Commissioner for Northern Ireland has approved and applied the *obiter* suggestion of Judge Ward in *PL v SSWP (JSA)* [2013] UKUT 227 (AA) (on the pre-October 2012 form of the Great Britain legislation) that in deciding whether a claimant had good cause of failing to avail himself of a reasonable opportunity of a place on a training scheme or employment programme a tribunal erred in law, where the circumstances raised the issue, in the failing to consider the appropriateness of the particular scheme or programme to the claimant in the light of his skills and experience and previous attendance on any placements. Judge Ward's suggestion had been that the test was whether the claimant had reasonably considered that what was provided would not help him. It seems likely that a similar general approach will be taken to issues of "good reason" under s.19A(2)(d)–(f). It may though still need to be sorted out how far the issue turns on the claimant's subjective view, within the bounds of reasonableness, in the light of the information provided at the time, as against a tribunal's view of the appropriateness of what was to be provided. The Chief Commissioner made no comment on the treatment of the claimant's refusal to complete and sign forms with information about criminal convictions and health, that the First-tier Tribunal had found were reasonably required by the training provider as part of its application process for the scheme, as a failure by the claimant to avail himself of a reasonable opportunity of a place on the training scheme. **3.008.1**

p.161, *annotation to the State Pension Credit Regulations 2002 (SI 2002/1792) reg.4 (Exclusions)*

In *SJ v Secretary of State for Work and Pensions (SPC)* [2015] UKUT 0505 (AAC) the claimant had initially entered the UK under a sponsorship agreement. She then applied for indefinite leave to remain (ILR) under para.317 of the Immigration Rules as a parent of a person present and settled in the UK. A First-tier Tribunal (Immigration and Asylum Chamber) allowed her appeal both under the Immigration Rules and on human rights grounds. The Home Office later granted the claimant ILR, after which she applied for pension credit. The claim was refused on the basis that the claimant was not entitled to pension credit for five years from the date the sponsorship undertaking had been signed. The First- **3.009** tier Tribunal (Social Entitlement Chamber) refused the claimant's appeal. The claimant's representative argued that her grant of ILR was made on human rights grounds, and was not premised on the sponsorship undertaking, so she was not a person subject to immigration control. Judge Wikeley dismissed the appeal, concluding that the Home Office decision was one under the Immigration Rules as opposed to human rights grounds. The case was distinguished from *R(PC)* 1/09, where the Home Office had made a decision to grant ILR outside the Immigration Rules. Thus the claimant was a person subject to immigration control and not entitled to state pension credit.

p.196, *introductory note to the Jobseekers (Back to Work Schemes) Act 2013*

3.010   The appeals to the Court of Appeal against the decisions of Lang J in *R. (Reilly (No.2) and Hewstone) v SSWP* [2014] EWHC 2182 Admin [2015] Q.B. 573 and of the three-judge panel of the Upper Tribunal in *SSWP v TJ (JSA)* [2015] UKUT 56 (AAC) were heard together on November 24, 2015. It is hoped that if the court's reserved decision is handed down before this Supplement goes to press a summary can be included.

p.199, *introductory note to the Jobseekers (Back to Work Schemes) Act 2013*

3.011   There have been several further official reports on sanctions policy (extending beyond those under s.17A of the old style Jobseekers Act 1995) since those mentioned in the main volume, in particular the House of Commons Work and Pensions Committee, *Benefits Sanctions policy beyond the Oakley Review,* HC 814 2014–15 (March 24, 2015), *Benefit Sanctions: Beyond the Oakley Review: Government Response to the Committee's Fifth Report of Session 2014–15,* HC 557 2015-16 (October 22, 2015) and subsequent letters between the Secretary of State and the chairman of the Committee. There is an excellent summary of this and other literature from many sources as at November 30, 2015 in a House of Commons Debate Pack on Benefit Sanctions produced by the House of Commons Library (CDP–0113). The Scottish Government has also issued a number of updates on benefit sanctions in Scotland.

p.280, *annotation to the Income Support (General) Regulations 1987 (SI 1978/1967) reg.12 (Relevant education)*

3.012   Note that the definition of "approved training" in reg.1(3) of the Child Benefit (General) Regulations 2006 was amended with effect from August 31, 2015 by the Child Benefit (General) (Amendment) Regulations 2015 (SI 2015/1512). The amendments included deleting sub-para.(a) of the definition. This is because the two programmes, "Foundation Learning" and "Access to Apprenticeships", named in sub-para.(a) are no longer available. The consequence is that there are now no programmes specified for the purposes of the definition of "approved training" in England but according to the Explanatory Memorandum which accompanies SI 2015/1512 a study programme under s.4 of the Education and Skills Act 2008 also includes "Traineeship".

pp.344–345, *annotation to the Income Support (General) Regulations 1987 (SI 1987/1967) reg.21AA (Special cases: supplemental—Persons from abroad—The right to reside from April 30, 2006—Extended right of residence—"Workseekers" and "Jobseekers"—The decision in SSWP v RR (IS))*

In *RO v SSWP (JSA)* [2015] UKUT 533 (AAC), the UT confirms   3.013
that the decision of the three-judge panel in *SSWP v RR (IS)* [2013] UKUT 21 (AAC) is not authority for the broader proposition suggested by some of the language used in the earlier decision, namely that that all jobseekers who can bring themselves within art.39 of TEC are thereby workers for the purposes of art.7(1)(a) of the Citizenship Directive (see p.345 of the main volume).

pp.335–338, *annotation to the Income Support (General) Regulations 1987 (SI 1987/1967), reg.21AA (Special cases: supplemental—Persons from abroad—The right to reside from April 30, 2006—Extended right of residence—Persons who retain the status of worker— Pregnancy—Issues arising from the decision of the CJEU in* Saint Prix)

A number of legal and practical issues from the decision of the CJEU   3.014
in *Saint Prix v Secretary of State for Work and Pensions* (C-507/12) [2014] AACR 18, namely:

  (a) What is the nature of the *Saint Prix* right: in particular, is it a right to be assessed prospectively or retrospectively?

  (b) To whom is the *Saint Prix* right available?

  (c) When does a *Saint Prix* right start?

  (d) How long does the "reasonable period" last?

  (e) Does a woman have to return to work (or find another job) or will a return to seeking work suffice?

  (f) Can a *Saint Prix* right contribute to the period of time necessary to acquire the right of permanent residence under Art.16 of Directive 2004/38?

These have been considered by the Upper Tribunal in *SSWP v SFF, ADR v SSWP, CS v LB Barnet & SSWP* [2015] UKUT 502. Judge Ward answered those questions as follows:

  (a) The *Saint Prix* right is to be assessed prospectively. The proviso in para.(41) of the CJEU's judgment (quoted in full on p.337 of the main volume)—namely that in order to retain worker status a formerly-pregnant woman should "[return] to work or find another job within a reasonable period after confinement"—did not create "a condition precedent to the [*Saint Prix*] right coming into existence, which would have the consequence that the existence of the right could only be assessed retrospectively, but . . . a condition subsequent for terminating it where it is not met . . .".

The issue was "primarily one of the woman's intention, but subject to the special protection conferred by the CJEU's judgment". Approaching it in that way "means that a woman is protected by her worker status until such time, not exceeding the end of the "reasonable period" contemplated by [47] of *Saint-Prix*, as she by her words or actions shows an intention not to be part of the employment market": see para.22 of *SFF*. This approach avoids the potential problem with s.12(8)(b) of the Social Security Act 1998 that is noted on p.337 of the main volume.

(b) As is implicit in the CJEU's decision itself—and as was not in dispute in before the Upper Tribunal—the *Saint Prix* right is available to women who have exercised the right of freedom of movement for workers and have been employed in a Member State other than that of their residence and to those who by meeting the conditions of Article 7(3) retain worker status while looking for work. It has yet to be decided whether the right is available to a "jobseeker" in the EU sense—i.e., a woman who has never previously worked in the UK or who, having worked in the UK, has left the labour market but is now seeking work. That is because none of the claimants in *SFF* fell within that category.

(c) Judge Ward ruled that "the 11th week before the expected date of childbirth which appears as the earliest permitted commencement of a maternity pay period and for payment of maternity allowance and, more importantly, as the start of the period when a claimant for income support fulfils, without more, the requirement to fall within a "prescribed category" of person . . . provides a convenient yardstick by which to assess whether the test is fulfilled but one that is capable of being displaced in particular cases".

(d) Contrary to the guidance issued by the Secretary of State in DMG Memo 25/14—which had advised decision makers that the maximum reasonable period was the 26 weeks during which a woman is entitled to ordinary maternity leave—Judge Ward ruled that the reasonable period is to be determined taking account of the 52-week period covered by the rights to ordinary and additional maternity leave and of the circumstances of the particular case: see para.35. He added:

> "As a matter of practice rather than of law, it seems likely that it will be an unusual case in which the period is other than the 52 week period".

(e) A return to seeking work will suffice. Judge Ward accepted (at para.39) a submission from the Secretary of State, that:

> "if a woman with rights under Article 7(3)(b) or (c) had to find a job within the reasonable period after childbirth rather than merely returning to qualifying work seeking, then she would have to do more as the result of leaving the labour market temporarily because of pregnancy and the aftermath of childbirth than if she had remained as a person with retained worker status under Article 7(3)(b) or (c)."

The same was true of a woman who was in employment at the beginning of the reasonable period but whose job had come to an end during that period (para.40). The reference in the CJEU's judgment to a woman a condition that a woman "returns to work or finds another job" could be explained by the fact that that is what had happened on the facts of *Saint Prix* (para.41).

(f) The *Saint Prix* right does count towards the continuous period of legal residence necessary to acquire the right of permanent residence. The Secretary of State did not dispute that in *SFF* and therefore the reason why it is so is not explained. It is because a woman exercising the *Saint Prix* right retains worker status while she does so. Therefore, that period counts towards the qualifying residence period for the permanent right of residence in the same way as any other period of residence as a retained-status worker.

pp.338–339, *annotation to the Income Support (General) Regulations 1987 (SI 1987/1967), reg.21AA (Special cases: supplemental—Persons from abroad—The right to reside from April 30, 2006—Extended right of residence-Persons who retain the status of worker-Involuntary unemployment-Decision of the CJEU in Alimanovic)*

The judgment of the Grand Chamber of the CJEU in *Jobcenter Berlin Neukölln v Alimanovic* (C-67/14) was issued on September 15, 2015. In response to the questions referred by the *Bundessozialgericht* (German Federal Social Court) (which are set out on p.339 of the main volume), the Court ruled: **3.015**

"Article 24 of [the Citizenship Directive] and Article 4 of Regulation (EC) No 883/2004 of the European Parliament and of the Council of 29 April 2004 on the coordination of social security systems, as amended by Commission Regulation (EU) No 1244/2010 of 9 December 2010, must be interpreted as not precluding legislation of a Member State under which nationals of other Member States who are in a situation such as that referred to in Article 14(4)(b) of that directive are excluded from entitlement to certain 'special non-contributory cash benefits' within the meaning of Article 70(2) of Regulation No 883/2004, which also constitute 'social assistance' within the meaning of Article 24(2) of Directive 2004/38, although those benefits are granted to nationals of the Member State concerned who are in the same situation."

p.380, *annotation to Income Support Regulations 1988 (SI 1987/1967), reg.21AA (Special cases: supplemental—persons from abroad—The right to reside from April 30, 2006—Compatibility of the right to reside test with EU law—Decision of the Supreme Court in* Mirga)

The judgment of the Supreme Court in *Mirga v Secretary of State for Work and Pensions* [2016] UKSC 1 was given on January 27, 2016. The Court upheld the decision on the Court of Appeal (which is noted in the main volume). On the issue of proportionality, the Court decided,   **3.016** following the judgments of the CJEU in *Dano v Jobcenter Leipzig* (C-333/13) and *Jobcenter Berlin Neukölln v Alimanovic* (Case C-67/14), that the provisions of Directive 2004/38/EC "guarantees a significant level of legal certainty and transparency in the context of the award of social assistance by way of basic provision while complying with the principle of proportionality" so that an examination of proportionality in the context of an individual case was not necessary, except (possibly) in exceptional cases, of which Ms Mirga's case was not one.

In *Pensionsversicherungsanstalt v Brey* (Case C-140/12) the CJEU had held that (in the circumstances of that case) it was necessary for a host member States to carry out individual assessment of whether allowing a claim for social assistance by a national of another EEA State would amount to a burden on the social assistance system of the host member State before it could refuse that claim (see pp.348–50 of the main volume). Taken together with the judgments in *Dano*, and *Alimanovic*, the Supreme Court's judgment in *Mirga* raises the issue—which will need to be explored in other cases—of whether any circumstances remain in which the *Brey* requirement continues to apply.

pp.483–487, *annotation to the Income Support (General) Regulations 1987 (SI 1987/1967) reg.46 (Calculation of capital—"claimant holding as trustee")*

3.017   *DF v Secretary of State (ESA)* [2015] UKUT 611 (AAC) concerns the question of whether a claimant can argue that he is not the beneficial owner of the funds in an Individual Savings Account (ISA) that is in his name. One of the conditions for an ISA account is that money invested in the account is in the beneficial ownership of the account holder (see reg.4(6) of the ISA Regulations 1998).

Mr F maintained that the money in his ISA account really belonged to his daughter and that it was not part of his capital because he had no beneficial interest in it. His daughter confirmed this in a letter. The ISA was designed to keep her money away from an unreliable partner.

The Secretary of State argued that the decision in *CIS/2836/2006* prevented Mr F from raising this beneficial interest argument. A person in whose name an ISA is held has to be regarded as the beneficial owner of the money in the account. While *CIS/2836/2006* concerned the Personal Equity Plan Regulations 1989, the ISA Regulations 1998 were said to be identical.

Judge Mitchell, however, concludes that *CIS/2836/2006* is restricted to "presumption of advancement" cases, i.e., cases in which the money is given by someone standing *in loco parentis* to a child, or by a husband to a wife, where there is a presumption that a gift was intended (note that the presumption of advancement is due to be abolished by s.199 of the Equality Act 2010 but this section has not yet come into force). To the extent that *CIS/2836/2006* could be read as going further, in his view it was not consistent with the House of Lords' decision in *Tinsley v Milligan* [1994] 1 A.C. 34.

Furthermore, Judge Mitchell holds that *CIS/2836/2006* did not decide that ISA-type legislation operates to extinguish beneficial interests of third parties in ISA deposits. Neither the ISA Regulations 1998 nor the enabling power under which they were made (s.333(2) Income and Corporation Taxes Act 1988) had the effect of altering existing rights in relation to property. The legislation was only concerned with creating a special account with special tax advantages.

Judge Mitchell goes on to reject the Secretary of State's argument that the law of illegality meant that, as a matter of public policy, a claimant could not rely on a beneficial interest that s/he had previously denied. This was inconsistent with the Supreme Court's decision in *Hounga v Allen* [2014] UKSC 47; [2014] 1 W.L.R. 2889 and the Court of Appeal's decision in *R (Best) v Secretary of State for Justice* (Rev 1) [2015] EWCA Civ 17. In his view it was better for a First-tier Tribunal in an ISA case to ignore the role that may or may not be played by the law of illegality and to simply focus on whether it accepted that the beneficial interest in the funds lay elsewhere.

Judge Mitchell does, however, point out the risks that a claimant runs   3.018 if s/he argues that a third party has a beneficial interest in the sums deposited in an ISA, namely, conceding that any ISA tax reliefs were improperly awarded and the possibility of criminal proceedings for a tax offence under s.106A Taxes Management Act 1970 (see para.17 of the decision).

Finally Judge Mitchell states that if a claimant does argue that the beneficial interest in an ISA lies elsewhere, the original ISA agreement and the declaration signed by the claimant that all the money deposited belongs to him/her (see reg.12(3) of the ISA Regulations 1998) should be obtained. Findings of fact will then need to be made to resolve the dispute as to beneficial ownership. Judge Mitchell comments that the "claimant may well have an evidential mountain to climb".

In *MC v SSWP (IS)* [2015] UKUT 600 (AAC) the claimant had saved up her daughters' disability living allowance in an account in the claimant's name. A tribunal accepted that in relation to an earlier period the claimant was holding the money on trust for her daughters. However, when she used a substantial part of the money to meet rent arrears, the tribunal considered that this suggested that what was previously held on trust had been subsequently "converted" into the claimant's capital by her actions. Judge Wikeley holds, however, accepting the Secretary of State's arguments, that this was wrong in law. Firstly, as the claimant had been made an appointee by DWP to act on behalf of her daughters in benefit matters, she was acting as a *de facto* trustee. Secondly, this was an obvious example of an informal trust over money, created without any legal formalities. Thirdly, paying off rent arrears helped to keep a roof over the daughters' heads and was a perfectly reasonable use of their savings, consistent with the purposes of the trust.

p.511, *annotation to the Income Support (General) Regulations 1987 (SI 1987/1967)*

VW v SSWP (IS) [2015] UKUT 51 (AAC) is to be reported as [2015]   3.018.1 AACR 39.

pp.610–611, *amendment to the Income Support (General) Regulations 1987 (SI 1987/1967) Sch.2 para.13 (Severe disability premium)*

3.019   With effect from November 4, 2015, reg.14 of the Universal Credit and Miscellaneous Amendments Regulations 2015 (SI 2015/1754) amended para.13 to read as follows:

Severe Disability Premium

13.—(1) The condition is that the claimant is a severely disabled person. (2) For the purposes of sub-paragraph (1), a claimant shall be treated as being a severely disabled person if, and only if—

    (a) in the case of a single claimant, a lone parent or a claimant who is treated as having no partner in consequence of sub-paragraph (2A)—

        (i) he is in receipt of attendance allowance, the care component of disability living allowance at the highest or middle rate prescribed in accordance with section 37ZB(3) of the Social Security Act or the daily living component of personal independence payment at the standard or enhanced rate in accordance with section 78(3) of the 2012 Act or armed forces independence payment, and

        (ii) subject to sub-paragraph (3), he has no non-dependants aged 18 or over normally residing with him or with whom he is normally residing, and

        (iii) no person is entitled to, and in receipt of, a carer's allowance under section 70 of the Contributions and Benefits Act [or has an award of universal credit which includes the carer element] in respect of caring for him;

    (b) in the case of a claimant who has a partner—

        (i) he is in receipt of attendance allowance, the care component of disability living allowance at the highest or middle rate prescribed in accordance with section 37ZB(3) of the Social Security Act or the daily living component of personal independence payment at the standard or enhanced rate in accordance with section 78(3) of the 2012 Act or armed forces independence payment; and

        (ii) his partner is also in receipt of such an allowance or, if he is a member of a polygamous marriage, all the partners of that marriage are in receipt thereof; and

        (iii) subject to sub-paragraph (3), he has no non-dependants aged 18 or over normally residing with him or with whom he is normally residing,

and either a person is entitled to, and in receipt of, a carer's allowance [or has an award of universal credit which includes the carer element] in respect of caring for only one of the couple or, in the case of a polygamous marriage, for one or more but not all the partners of the marriage or, as the case may be, no person is entitled to, and in receipt of, such an allowance [or has such an award of universal credit] in respect of caring for either member of the couple or any partner of the polygamous marriage.

(2A) Where a claimant has a partner who does not satisfy the condition in sub-paragraph (2)(b)(ii), and that partner is severely sight impaired or blind or treated as severely sight impaired or blind within the meaning of paragraph 12(1)(a)(iii) and (2), that partner shall be treated for the purposes of sub-paragraph (2) as if he were not a partner of the claimant.

(3A) For the purposes of sub-paragraph (2)(a)(ii) and (2)(b)(iii) no account shall be taken of—

(a) a person receiving attendance allowance, . . . the care component of disability living allowance at the highest or middle rate prescribed in accordance with section 37ZB(3) of the Social Security Act [SSCBA, s.72(3)] or the daily living component of personal independence payment at the standard or enhanced rate in accordance with section 78(3) of the 2012 Act or armed forces independence payment; or

(b) . . .

(c) subject to sub-paragraph (4), a person who joins the claimant's household for the first time in order to care for the claimant or his partner and immediately before so joining the claimant or his partner was treated as a severely disabled person; or

(d) a person who is severely sight impaired or blind or treated as severely sight impaired or blind within the meaning of paragraph 12(1)(a)(iii) and (2).

(3) For the purposes of sub-paragraph (2)(b) a person shall be treated

(a) as being in receipt of attendance allowance, or the care component of disability living allowance at the highest or middle rate prescribed in accordance with section 37ZB(3) of the Social Security Act [SSCBA, s.72(3)] if he would, but for his being a patient for a period exceeding 28 days, be so in receipt;

(b) as being entitled to and in receipt of a carer's allowance [or having an award of universal credit which includes the carer element] if he would, but for the person for whom he was caring being a patient in hospital for a period exceeding 28 days, be so entitled and in receipt [of carer's allowance or have such an award of universal credit].

(c) as being in receipt of the daily living component of personal independence payment at the standard or enhanced rate in accordance with section 78(3) of the 2012 Act if he would, but for a suspension of benefit in accordance with regulations under section 86(1) (hospital in-patients) of the 2012 Act, be so in receiPt

(3ZA) For the purposes of sub-paragraph (2)(a)(iii) and (2)(b), no account shall be taken of an award of a carer's allowance [or universal credit which includes the carer element] to the extent that payment of such an award is backdated for a period before the date on which the award is first paid.

(4) Sub-paragraph (3)(c) shall apply only for the first 12 weeks following the date on which the person to whom that provision applies first joins the claimant's household.

(5) In sub-paragraph (2)(a)(iii) and (b), references to a person being in receipt of a carer's allowance [or as having an award of universal credit which includes the carer element] shall include references to a person who would have been in receipt of that allowance [or had such an award] but for the application of a restriction under section 6B or 7 of the Social Security Fraud Act 2001 (loss of benefit provisions).

[(6) For the purposes of this paragraph, a person has an award of universal credit which includes the carer element if the person has an award of universal credit which includes an amount which is the carer element under regulation 29 of the Universal Credit Regulations 2013.]

pp.624–626, *annotation to the Income Support (General) Regulations 1987 (SI 1987/1967) Sch.2 para.13 (Severe disability premium)*

3.020 The effect of the amendments made with effect from November 4, 2015 to para.13 (and to paras 15 and 20I of Sch.1 to the JSA Regulations 1996 and para.6 of Sch.4 to the ESA Regulations 2008) by SI 2015/1754 is that where a person's universal credit includes the carer element (see Vol.V), the severely disabled person for whom s/he cares will not be entitled to a severe disability premium.

pp.704–706, *annotation to the Income Support (General) Regulations 1987 (SI 1987/1967) Sch.3 (Housing costs) para.17 (Other housing costs)*

3.021 *Liverpool City Council v (1) NM, (2) WD (HB)* [2015] UKUT 523 (AAC) holds that service charges for the supply of water for communal areas in sheltered or supported accommodation are eligible for housing benefit (and thus are not excluded under para.17(2)(b)), except for water used for the provision of laundry which is ineligible under para. 1(a)(ii) of Sch.1 to the Housing Benefit Regulations 2006. But water charges for the cleaning of a communal laundry is eligible (see para. 1(a)(iv)(aa) of Sch.1); this would include the cleaning of laundry equipment (see para.1(a)(ii)).

M was a licensee of a room in a supported housing scheme for 16–25 year olds. D was an assured tenant in a sheltered housing scheme for those over 55 and for younger people with disabilities. In both cases their service charges for water rates were broken down into communal water charges, which were stated to be "eligible for HB", and charges for personal use of water (in their room/flat), which were stated to be "not eligible for HB".

The Council disallowed housing benefit in respect of the communal water charges. A tribunal allowed the claimants' appeals and the Council appealed to the Upper Tribunal.

Judge Knowles QC firstly rejects the Council's submission that the accommodation occupied by M was not "sheltered accommodation" within the meaning of that term in para.8 of Sch.1 to the Housing Benefit Regulations 2006. Applying the Court of Appeal's decision in

Oxford City Council v Basey [2012] EWCA Civ 115 "sheltered accommodation" was "an inherently flexible concept" and included accommodation, such as in M's case, where the accommodation was provided on the basis that the licensee accepted support services. The consequence was that if communal water charges were eligible for housing benefit, this would include charges for water use in halls, passageways *and* rooms of common use in both M's and D's accommodation.

In relation to the water charges, the Council contended that all water charges, whether for personal or communal use, fell to be deducted under reg.12(B)(5) of the Housing Benefit Regulations 2006. It also contended that communal water charges were ineligible service charges in accordance with Sch.1 because they were either for "day-to-day living expenses" within the meaning of para.1(a) or charges which were not connected with the provision of adequate accommodation within the meaning of para.1(g). **3.022**

Judge Knowles holds that reg.12(B)(5) was only concerned with the deduction of water charges for personal use when the claimant is not separately billed. It has no application to communal water charges. She also rejected the contention that communal water charges were "day-to-day living expenses" and found that they were clearly charges related to the provision of adequate accommodation, applying the decision in *CIS/1460/1995*.

The appeals were remitted to a differently constituted tribunal because the original tribunal had not determined the proportion of the communal water charges attributable to laundry use (which was ineligible) and had calculated the claimants' personal water charges in accordance with reg.12B(5)(c) when the correct provision in the circumstances was reg.12B(5)(b).

pp.838–839, *General note to the Social Security (Immigration and Asylum) Consequential Amendments Regulations 2000 (SI 2000/636)— Commentary on s.119(5)(c) of the Immigration and Asylum Act 1999 (A person who has leave to enter or remain which was given as a result of a maintenance undertaking)*

At the end of para.2.1141 on p.839 add "The position is different where the decision to grant leave was made under the Immigration Rules: see *CSPC/379/2009* and *SJ v SSWP (SPC)* [2015] UKUT 0505 (AAC)." **3.023**

p.840, *annotation to the Social Security (Immigration and Asylum) Consequential Amendments Regulations 2000 (SI 2000/636) reg.2(1) and Sch. Pt 1 (Persons not excluded from specified benefits under section 115 of the Immigration and Asylum Act 1999: The ECSMA Agreement and the European Social Charter)*

At the end of the first sentence of para.2.1144 add "if they are "lawfully present in the United Kingdom". For an example, see *OD v SSWP (JSA)* [2015] UKUT 0438 (AAC)." **3.024**

p.1066, *annotation to reg.25 of the JSA Regulations 1996 (Entitlement ceasing on a failure to comply with certain requirements under regs 23 to 24)*

3.025   In relation to a failure to comply with a requirement under reg.24(6) and (10) to provide a signed declaration (see reg.25(1)(c)), Judge Hemingway in *KH v SSWP (JSA)* [2015] UKUT 497 (AAC) applied the exception to reg.25(1)(c) in reg.27 without consideration of the convincing reasoning of Mr Commissioner Stockman in *LDG v DSD (JSA)* [2015] NICom 15 (as mentioned in the main volume) that the part of reg.27 concerning showing good cause for the failure to comply is not valid. See the entry for p.1071 for more details.

p.1071, *annotation to reg.27 of the JSA Regulations 1996 (Where entitlement is not to cease under reg.25(1)(c))*

3.026   In *KH v SSWP (JSA)* [2015] UKUT 497 (AAC) Judge Hemingway set aside a decision of a First-tier Tribunal for failing to give proper consideration to whether a letter received from the claimant within five days of failing to provide a signed declaration under reg.24(6) and (10) might have contained information relevant to whether she had a good reason for the failure, so as, according to the terms of reg.27, to prevent the termination of entitlement under reg.25(1)(c). However, he had not been referred to and did not take into account the convincing reasoning of Mr Commissioner Stockman in *LDG v DSD (JSA)* [2015] NICom 15 (see the main volume) that the requirement in reg.27 for a claimant to show a good reason for the failure to provide the signed declaration, in addition to making contact with an employment officer within the five days, is not valid. The judge was inclined to say that the claimant's letter (which was not in the papers before him) was, in the absence of any submission to the contrary from the Secretary of State, a making of contact in the manner set out in the relevant notification under reg.23. Thus, if the reasoning in *LDG* had been adopted, he might well have been able to substitute a decision in the claimant's favour, rather than remit the case to a new tribunal for rehearing. In view of the complete lack of any reference to *LDG*, the decision in *KH* should not be taken as in any way undermining the force and authority of the reasoning in *LDG*.

Judge Hemingway rightly criticised the apparent lack of care in the decision-making process and in the presentation of the case to the First-tier Tribunal, in failing to provide copies of potentially relevant documents or of a decision under appeal. He stressed that "decisions which result in a claimant ceasing to have income can have potentially very serious consequences such that considerable care ought to be taken at all stages in the decision-making process and the explanation of that process once an appeal is lodged."

p.1100, *annotation to the Jobseeker's Allowance Regulations 1996 (SI 1996/207) reg.54 (Relevant education)*

3.027   See the note to reg.12 of the Income Support (General) Regulations 1987 in this Updater.

pp.1276–1277, *amendment to the Jobseeker's Allowance Regulations 1996 (SI 1996/207) Sch.1 para.15 (Severe disability premium)*

With effect from November 4, 2015, reg.15(1) and (2) of the Univer-   3.028
sal Credit and Miscellaneous Amendments Regulations 2015 (SI
2015/1754) amended para.15 to read as follows:

Severe disability premium

15.—(1) In the case of a single claimant, a lone parent or a claimant
who is treated as having no partner in consequence of sub-paragraph
(3), the condition is that—
  (a) he is in receipt of attendance allowance, the care component of
      disability living allowance at the highest or middle rate pre-
      scribed in accordance with section 72(3) of the Benefits Act,
      armed forces independence payment or the daily living compo-
      nent of personal independence payment at the standard or
      enhanced rate in accordance with section 78(3) of the 2012 Act;
      and
  (b) subject to sub-paragraph (4), there are no non-dependants aged
      18 or over normally residing with him or with whom he is
      normally residing; and
  (c) no person is entitled to, and in receipt of, a carer's allowance
      under section 70 of the Benefits Act [or has an award of univer-
      sal credit which includes the carer element] in respect of caring
      for him;
(2) Where the claimant has a partner, the condition is that—
  (a) the claimant is in receipt of attendance allowance, the care
      component of disability living allowance at the highest or mid-
      dle rate prescribed in accordance with section 72(3) of the
      Benefits Act, armed forces independence payment or the daily
      living component of personal independence payment at the
      standard or enhanced rate in accordance with section 78(3) of
      the 2012 Act; and
  (b) the partner is also in receipt of a qualifying benefit, or if he is a
      member of a polygamous marriage, all the partners of that
      marriage are in receipt of a qualifying benefit; and
  (c) subject to sub-paragraph (4), there is no non-dependant aged
      18 or over normally residing with him or with whom he is
      normally residing; and
  (d) either—
       (i) no person is entitled to, and in receipt of, a carer's allow-
           ance under section 70 of the Benefits Act [or has an award
           of universal credit which includes the carer element] in
           respect of caring for either member of the couple or all the
           members of the polygamous marriage; or
      (ii) a person is engaged in caring for one member (but not
           both members) of the couple, or one or more but not all
           members of the polygamous marriage, and in consequence
           is entitled to a carer's allowance under section 70 of the

Benefits Act [or has an award of universal credit which includes the carer element] .

(3) Where the claimant has a partner who does not satisfy the condition in subparagraph (2)(b), and that partner is severely sight impaired or blind or treated as severely sight impaired or blind within the meaning of paragraph 14(1)(h) and (2), that partner shall be treated for the purposes of sub-paragraph (2) as if he were not a partner of the claimant.

(4) The following persons shall not be regarded as a non-dependant for the purposes of sub-paragraphs (1)(b) and (2)(c)—

(a) a person in receipt of attendance allowance, the care component of disability living allowance at the highest or middle rate prescribed in accordance with section 72(3) of the Benefits Act, armed forces independence payment or the daily living component of personal independence payment at the standard or enhanced rate in accordance with section 78(3) of the 2012 Act;

(b) subject to sub-paragraph (6), a person who joins the claimant's household for the first time in order to care for the claimant or his partner and immediately before so joining the claimant or his partner satisfied the condition in sub-paragraph (1) or, as the case may be, (2);

(c) a person who is severely sight impaired or blind or treated as severely sight impaired or blind within the meaning of paragraph 14(1)(h) and (2).

(5) For the purposes of sub-paragraph (2), a person shall be treated.

(a) as being in receipt of attendance allowance, or the care component of disability living allowance at the highest or middle rate prescribed in accordance with section 72(3) of the Benefits Act if he would, but for his being a patient for a period exceeding 28 days, be so in receipt;

(aa) as being in receipt of the daily living component of personal independence payment at the standard or enhanced rate in accordance with section 78 of the 2012 Act if he would, but for regulations made under section 86(1) (hospital in-patients) of the 2012 Act, be so in receipt;

(b) as being entitled to and in receipt of a carer's allowance [or having an award of universal credit which includes the carer element] if he would, but for the person for whom he was caring being a patient in hospital for a period exceeding 28 days, be so entitled and in receipt [of carer's allowance or have such an award of universal credit] .

(6) Sub-paragraph (4)(b) shall apply only for the first 12 weeks following the date on which the person to whom that provision applies first joins the claimant's household.

(7) For the purposes of sub-paragraph (1)(c) and (2)(d), no account shall be taken of an award of carer's allowance [or universal credit which includes the carer element] to the extent that payment of such

an award is backdated for a period before the date on which the award is first paid.

(8) A person shall be treated as satisfying this condition if he would have satisfied the condition specified for a severe disability premium in income support in paragraph 13 of Schedule 2 to the Income Support Regulations by virtue only of regulations 4 to 6 of the Income Support (General) Amendment (No.6) Regulations 1991 (savings provisions in relation to severe disability premium) and for the purposes of determining whether in the particular case regulation 4 of those Regulations had ceased to apply in accordance with regulation 5(2)(a) of those Regulations, a person who is entitled to an income-based jobseeker's allowance shall be treated as entitled to income support.

(9) In sub-paragraphs (1)(c) and (2)(d), references to a person being in receipt of a carer's allowance [or as having an award of universal credit which includes the carer element] shall include references to a person who would have been in receipt of that allowance [or had such an award] but for the application of a restriction under section 6B or 7 of the Social Security Fraud Act 2001 (loss of benefit provisions).

[(10) For the purposes of this paragraph, a person has an award of universal credit which includes the carer element if the person has an award of universal credit which includes an amount which is the carer element under regulation 29 of the Universal Credit Regulations 2013.]

pp.1282–1293, *amendment to the Jobseeker's Allowance Regulations 1996 (SI 1996/207) Sch.1 para.20I (Severe disability premium)*

With effect from November 4, 2015, reg.15(1) and (3) of the Universal Credit and Miscellaneous Amendments Regulations 2015 (SI 2015/1754) amended para.20I to read as follows: 3.029

Severe disability premium

20I.—(1) The condition is that—
  (a) a member of a joint-claim couple is in receipt of attendance allowance, the care component of disability living allowance at the highest or middle rate prescribed in accordance with section 72(3) of the Benefits Act, armed forces independence payment or the daily living component of personal independence payment at the standard or enhanced rate in accordance with section 78(3) of the 2012 Act; and
  (b) the other member is also in receipt of such an allowance, or if he is a member of a polygamous marriage, all the partners of that marriage are in receipt of a qualifying benefit; and
  (c) subject to sub-paragraph (3), there is no non-dependant aged 18 or over normally residing with the joint-claim couple or with whom they are normally residing; and
  (d) either—

(i) no person is entitled to, and in receipt of, a carer's allowance under section 70 of the Benefits Act [or has an award of universal credit which includes the carer element] in respect of caring for either member or the couple or all the members of the polygamous marriage; or

(ii) a person is engaged in caring for one member (but not both members) of the couple, or one or more but not all members of the polygamous marriage, and in consequence is entitled to a carer's allowance under section 70 of the Benefits Act [or has an award of universal credit which includes the carer element] .

(2) Where the other member does not satisfy the condition in sub-paragraph (1)(b), and that member is severely sight impaired or blind or treated as severely sight impaired or blind within the meaning of paragraph 20H(1)(i) and (2), that member shall be treated for the purposes of sub-paragraph (1) as if he were not a member of the couple.

(3) The following persons shall not be regarded as non-dependant for the purposes of subparagraph (1)(c)—

(a) a person in receipt of attendance allowance, the care component of disability living allowance at the highest or middle rate prescribed in accordance with section 72(3) of the Benefits Act, armed forces independence payment or the daily living component of personal independence payment at the standard or enhanced rate in accordance with section 78(3) of the 2012 Act;

(b) subject to sub-paragraph (5), a person who joins the joint-claim couple's household for the first time in order to care for a member of a joint claim couple and immediately before so joining, that member satisfied the condition in sub-paragraph (1);

(c) a person who is severely sight impaired or blind or treated as severely sight impaired or blind within the meaning of paragraph 20H(1)(i) and (2).

(4) For the purposes of sub-paragraph (1), a member of a joint-claim couple shall be treated—

(a) as being in receipt of attendance allowance, or the care component of disability living allowance at the highest or middle rate prescribed in accordance with section 72(3) of the Benefits Act if he would, but for his being a patient for a period exceeding 28 days, be so in receipt;

(b) as being entitled to and in receipt of a carer's allowance [or having an award of universal credit which includes the carer element] if he would, but for the person for whom he was caring being a patient in hospital for a period exceeding 28 days, be so entitled and in receipt [of carer's allowance or have such an award of universal credit] .

(c) as being in receipt of the daily living component of personal independence payment at the standard or enhanced rate in accordance with section 78 of the 2012 Act if he would, but for regulations made under section 86(1) (hospital in-patients) of the 2012 Act, be so in receiPt

(5) Sub-paragraph (3)(b) shall apply only for the first 12 weeks following the date on which the person to whom that provision applies first joins the joint-claim couple's household.

(6) For the purposes of sub-paragraph (1)(d), no account shall be taken of an award of carer's allowance [or universal credit which includes the carer element] to the extent that payment of such an award is back-dated for a period before the date on which the award is first paid.

(7) In sub-paragraph (1)(d), the reference to a person being in receipt of a carer's allowance [or as having an award of universal credit which includes the carer element] shall include a reference to a person who would have been in receipt of that allowance [or had such an award] but for the application of a restriction under section 6B or 7 of the Social Security Fraud Act 2001 (loss of benefit provisions).

[(8) For the purposes of this paragraph, a person has an award of universal credit which includes the carer element if the person has an award of universal credit which includes an amount which is the carer element under regulation 29 of the Universal Credit Regulations 2013.]

p.1373, *annotation to the Jobseeker's Allowance (SAPOE) Regulations 2013*

An appeal currently before the Upper Tribunal (*CJSA/3205/2014* and *3206/2014*), in which an oral hearing is scheduled for January 2016, raises the issues of whether a revision after February 12, 2013 of an earlier invalid notice under the JSA (ESES) Regulations 2011 can be valid under the SAPOE Regulations and of whether the pro forma notice used specified enough information to satisfy reg.5(2). 3.030

pp.1392–1395, *annotation to the State Pension Credit Regulations 2002 (SI 2002/1792) reg.2 (Persons not in Great Britain)*

For an illustration of a case in which self-employed was found to be "marginal and ancillary" (the claimant was self-publishing his life story) rather than "genuine and effective", see *SSWP v HH (SPC)* [2015] UKUT 0583 (AAC). 3.031

p.1398, *amendment to the State Pension Credit Regulations 2002 (SI 2002/1792) reg.6 (Amount of the guarantee credit)*

With effect from November 4, 2015, reg.19(2) of the Universal Credit and Miscellaneous Amendments Regulations 2015 (SI 2015/1754) amended sub-para.(5)(b) by inserting ", or has an award of universal credit which includes the carer element under regulation 29 of the Universal Credit Regulations 2013," after the words "1992 Act". 3.032

p.1433, *amendment to the State Pension Credit Regulations 2002 (SI 2002/1792) Sch.1, para.1 (Circumstances in which persons are treated as being or not being severely disabled)*

3.033   With effect from November 4, 2015, reg.19(3) of the Universal Credit and Miscellaneous Amendments Regulations 2015 (SI 2015/1754) amended para.1 by (a) inserting ", or has an award of universal credit which includes the carer element," in sub-para.(1)(a)(iii) after the words "(carer's allowance)"; (b) in the closing words of sub-para.(1)(b) inserting ", or has an award of universal credit which includes the carer element," after the words "under section 70 of the 1992 Act" and "under section 70, or has an award of universal credit which includes the carer element," after the words "such an allowance"; (c) in sub-para.(1)(c)(iv) inserting ", or has an award of universal credit which includes the carer element, in" after the words "1992 Act"; (d) in sub-para.(2)(c) inserting ", or as having an award of universal credit which includes the carer element," after the words "1992 Act"; and (e) inserting after sub-para.(3) a new sub-para.(4)—

"(4) For the purposes of this paragraph, a person has an award of universal credit which includes the carer element if the person has an award of universal credit which includes an amount which is the carer element under regulation 29 of the Universal Credit Regulations 2013."

p.1437, *annotation to the State Pension Credit Regulations 2002 (SI 2002/1792) Sch.1 para.1 (Circumstances in which persons are treated as being or not being severely disabled)*

3.034   A "co-owner" who falls within the terms of para.2(6) is a person residing with the claimant whose presence is ignored for the purpose of para.1(1)(a)(ii). There is no definition in the Regulations of "co-owner". In *Secretary of State v HB (SPC)* [2015] UKUT 0389 (AAC) the claimant had been registered joint proprietor of the family home with her son. The claimant was later taken off the legal title, in order to facilitate a re-mortgage by the son in order to fund adaptations to the property for the severely disabled granddaughter. However, a deed of trust drawn up so that the claimant remained beneficially entitled to half the net profit of any sale. Judge Mark dismissed the Secretary of State's appeal from the tribunal's finding that the claimant remained a co-owner of the property: "There is no obvious reason, in deciding whether to award the severe disablement payment, for distinguishing between a case where the property is held on trust for the two occupants by some other person and one where the occupants or one of them holds the property on trust for the two of them" (para.10).

p.1452, *annotation to the State Pension Credit Regulations 2002 (SI 2002/1792) Sch.2 para.1 (housing costs)*

3.035   On the meaning of "co-owner", see *Secretary of State v HB (SPC)* [2015] UKUT 0389 (AAC) at para.12: "there is no apparent reason to distinguish in this respect between a legal and beneficial co-owner".

p.1452, *annotation to the State Pension Credit Regulations 2002 (SI 2002/1792) Sch.2 para.13 (other housing costs)*

The broad definition of "co-ownership scheme" in para.13(6)(a) "is a   3.036
clear indication that "co-owner" is intended in these Regulations to have
a wide meaning and not be confined to legal ownership as opposed to
beneficial ownership" (para.13).

pp.1485–1487, *amendment to the Social Fund Cold Weather Payments (General) Regulations 1988 (SI 1988/1724) Sch.1 (Identification of stations and postcode districts)*

With effect from November 1, 2015, reg.2(1) of and Sch.1 to the   3.037
Social Fund Cold Weather Payments (General) Amendment (No.2)
Regulations 2015 (SI 2015/1662) substituted the following for Sch.1:

Regulation 2(1)(a),(2) and 2(1A)

[SCHEDULE 1

IDENTIFICATION OF STATIONS AND POSTCODE DISTRICTS

Column (1)	*Column (2)*
Meteorological Office Station	*Postcode Districts*
1. Aberporth	SA35–48, SA64–65.
2. Aboyne No 2	AB30–34, AB38, AB51–55, DD8–9.
3. Albemarle	DH1–7, DH9, DL4–5, DL14–17, NE1–13, NE15–18, NE20–21, NE23, NE 25–46, SR1–7, TS21, TS28–29.
4. Andrewsfield	CB1–5, CB10–11, CB21–25, CM1–9, CM11–24, CM77, CO9, RM4, SG8–11.
5. Auchincruive	DG9, KA1–26, KA28–30, PA20.
6. Aultbea No 2	IV21–22, IV26.
7. Aviemore	AB37, IV13, PH19–26.
8. Bainbridge	BD23–24, DL8, DL11–13.
9. Bedford	MK1–19, MK40–46, NN1–16, NN29, PE19, SG5–7, SG15–19.
10. Bingley, No 2	BB4, BB8–12, BB18, BD1–22, HD3, HD7–9, HX1–7, LS21, LS29, OL13–14, S36.
11. Boscombe Down	BA12, RG28, SO20–23, SP1–5, SP7, SP9–11.
12. Braemar No 2	AB35–36, PH10–11, PH18.

Column (1)	Column (2)
Meteorological Office Station	*Postcode districts*
13. Brize Norton	OX1–6, OX8, OX10–14, OX18, OX20, OX25–29, OX33, OX44, SN7.
14. Capel Curig No 3	LL24–25, LL41.
15. Cardinham, Bodmin	PL13–18, PL22–35, TR9.
16. Carlisle	CA1–8, DG12, DG16.
17. Cassley	IV27–28, KW11, KW13.
18. Charlwood	BN5–6, BN44, GU5–6, ME6, ME14–20, RH1–20, TN1–20, TN22, TN27.
19. Charterhall	NE71, TD1–6, TD8, TD10–15.
20. Chivenor	EX23, EX31–34, EX39.
21. Coleshill	B1–21, B23–38, B40, B42–50, B60–80, B90–98, CV1–12, CV21–23, CV31–35, CV37, CV47, DY1–14, LE10, WS1–15, WV1–16.
22. Crosby	CH41–49, CH60–66, FY1–8, L1–40, PR1–5, PR8–9, PR25–26.
23. Culdrose	TR1–8, TR10–20, TR26–27.
24. Dunkeswell Aerodrome	DT6–8, EX1–5, EX8–15, EX24, TA21.
25. Dunstaffnage	PA30–31, PA34–35, PA37–38, PA62–65, PA67–75, PA80.
26. Dyce	AB10–16, AB21–25, AB39, AB41–43.
27. Edinburgh, Gogarbank	EH1–42, EH47–49, EH51–55, FK1–7, FK9–10, KY3, KY11–12.
28. Eskdalemuir	DG3–4, DG10–11, DG13–14, ML12, TD7, TD9.
29. Filton	BS1–11, BS13–16, BS20–24, BS29–32, BS34–37, BS39–41, BS48–49, GL11–13, NP16, NP26.
30. Fylingdales	YO13, YO18, YO21-22, YO62.
31. Glasgow, Bishopton	G1–5, G11–15, G20–23, G31–34, G40–46, G51–53, G60–62, G64, G66, G69, G71–78, G81–84, ML4–5, PA1–19, PA21–27, PA32.
32. Gravesend, Broadness	BR5–8, CM0, DA1–18, ME1–5, ME7–8, RM1–3, RM5–20, SS0–17.
33. Hawarden Airport	CH1–8, LL11–14, SY14.

Column (1)	Column (2)
Meteorological Office Station	*Postcode districts*
34. Heathrow	BR1–4, CR0, CR2–9, E1–18, E20, EC1–4, EN1–5, EN7–11, HA0–9, IG1–11, KT1–24, N1–22, NW1–11, SE1–28, SL0, SL3, SM1–7, SW1–20, TW1–20, UB1–11, W1–14, WC1–2, WD1–2.
35. Hereford, Credenhill	GL1–6, GL10, GL14–20, GL50–53, HR1–9, NP7–8, NP15, NP25, SY8, WR1–11, WR13–15.
36. Herstmonceux, West End	BN7–8, BN20–24, BN26–27, TN21, TN31–40.
37. High Wycombe, HQ Air	HP5–23, HP27, OX9, OX39, OX49, RG9, SL7–9.
38. Hurn	BH1–25, BH31, DT1–2, DT11, SP6.
39. Isle of Portland	DT3–5.
40. Keele	CW1–3, CW5, CW12, ST1–8, ST11–12, ST14–21.
41. Kinloss	AB44–45, AB56, IV1–3, IV5, IV7–12, IV15–20, IV30–32, IV36.
42. Kirkwall	KW15–17.
43. Lake Vyrnwy No 2	LL20–21, LL23, SY10, SY15–17, SY19, SY21–22.
44. Langdon Bay	CT1–21, ME9–13, TN23–26, TN28–30.
45. Leconfield	DN14, HU1–20, YO11–12, YO14–17, YO25.
46. Leek, Thorncliffe	DE4, DE45, S32–33, SK13, SK17, SK22–23, ST9–10, ST13.
47. Lerwick	ZE1–3.
48. Leuchars	DD1–7, DD10–11, KY1–2, KY6–10, KY15–16, PH12, PH14.
49. Linton on Ouse	DL1–3, DL6–7, DL9–10, HG1–5, LS1–20, LS22–28, TS9, TS15–16, YO1, YO7–8, YO10, YO19, YO23–24, YO26, YO30–32, YO41–43, YO51, YO60–61.
50. Liscombe	EX16, EX35–36, TA22, TA24.
51. Little Rissington	CV36, GL54–56, OX7, OX15–17, WR12.
52. Llysdinam	LD1–8, SA19–20, SY7, SY9, SY18.
53. Loch Glascarnoch	IV4, IV6, IV14, IV23–24, IV63.
54. Loftus	SR8, TS1–8, TS10–14, TS17–20, TS22–27.
55. Machrihanish	KA27, PA28–29, PA41–49, PA60.

Column (1)	*Column (2)*
Meteorological Office Station	*Postcode districts*
56. Marham	CB6–7, IP24–28, PE12–14, PE30–38.
57. Mona	LL33–34, LL42–49, LL51–78.
58. Morpeth, Cockle Park	NE22, NE24, NE61–70.
59. North Wyke	EX6–7, EX17–22, EX37–38, PL19–21, TQ1–6, TQ9–14.
60. Nottingham, Watnall	CV13, DE1–3, DE5–7, DE11–15, DE21–24, DE55–56, DE65, DE72–75, LE1–9, LE11–14, LE16–19, LE65, LE67, NG1–22, NG25, NG31–34.
61. Pembrey Sands	SA1–8, SA14–18, SA31–34, SA61–63, SA66–73.
62. Plymouth, Mountbatten	PL1–12, TQ7–8.
63. Redesdale Camp	CA9, DH8, NE19, NE47–49.
64. Rhyl No 2	LL15–19, LL22, LL26–32.
65. Rochdale	BL0–9, M24, M26, OL1–12, OL15–16, SK15.
66. Rostherne No 2	CW4, CW6–11, M1–9, M11–23, M25, M27–35, M38, M40–41, M43–46, M50, M90, PR7, SK1–12, SK14, SK16, WA1–16, WN1–8.
67. Rothamsted	AL1–10, EN6, HP1–4, LU1–7, SG1–4, SG12–14, WD3–7, WD17–19, WD23–25.
68. St. Athan	CF3, CF5, CF10–11, CF14–15, CF23–24, CF31–36, CF61–64, CF71–72, NP10, NP18–20, SA10–13.
69. St. Bees Head No 2	CA13–15, CA18–28.
70. Salsburgh	EH43–46, G65, G67–68, ML1–3, ML6–11.
71. Scilly: St. Marys Airport	TR21–25.
72. Shap	CA10–12, CA16–17, LA8–10, LA21–23.
73. Shawbury	SY1–6, SY11–13, TF1–13.
74. Sheffield	DN1–8, DN11–12, HD1–2, HD4–6, S1–14, S17–18, S20–21, S25–26, S35, S40–45, S60–66, S70–75, S80–81, WF1–17.
75. Skye: Lusa	IV40–49, IV51–56, PH36, PH38–41.
76. South Farnborough	GU1–4, GU7–35, GU46–47, GU51–52, RG1–2, RG4–8, RG10, RG12, RG14, RG18–27, RG29–31, RG40–42, RG45, SL1–2, SL4–6, SO24.

Column (1)	Column (2)
Meteorological Office Station	*Postcode districts*
77. Stonyhurst	BB1–3, BB5–7, LA2, LA6–7, PR6.
78. Stornoway Airport	HS1–9.
79. Strathallan Airfield	FK8, FK11–19, G63, KY4–5, KY13–14, PH1–7, PH13.
80. Thorney Island	BN1–3, BN9–18, BN25, BN41–43, BN45, PO1–22, PO30–41, SO14–19, SO30–32, SO40–43, SO45, SO50–53.
81. Threave	DG1–2, DG5–8.
82. Tibenham Airfield	NR1–35.
83. Tiree	PA61, PA66, PA76–78, PH42–44.
84. Trawsgoed	LL35–40, SY20, SY23–25.
85. Tredegar, Bryn Bach Park No 2	CF37–48, CF81–83, NP4, NP11–13, NP22–24, NP44, SA9.
86. Tulloch Bridge	FK20–21, PA33, PA36, PA40, PH8–9, PH15–17, PH30–35, PH37, PH49–50.
87. Waddington	DN9–10, DN13, DN15–22, DN31–41, LN1–13, NG23–24, PE10–11, PE20–25.
88. Walney Island	LA1, LA3–5, LA11–20.
89. Wattisham	CB8–9, CO1–8, CO10–16, IP1–23, IP29–33.
90. Westonbirt	BA1–3, BA11, BA13–15, GL7–9, RG17, SN1–6, SN8–16, SN25–26.
91. Wick Airport	IV25, KW1–3, KW5–10, KW12, KW14.
92. Wittering	LE15, NN17–18, PE1–9, PE15–17, PE26–29.
93. Yeovilton	BA4–10, BA16, BA20–22, BS25–28, DT9–10, SP8, TA1–20, TA23.]

pp.1488–1489, *amendment to the Social Fund Cold Weather Payments (General) Regulations 1988 (SI 1988/1724) Sch.1 (Specified alternative stations)*

With effect from November 1, 2015, reg.2(2) of and Sch.2 to the Social Fund Cold Weather Payments (General) Amendment (No.2) Regulations 2015 (SI 2015/1662) substituted the following for Sch.2: **3.038**

Regulation 2(1), (1A) and (2)

[Schedule 2

SPECIFIED ALTERNATIVE STATIONS

Column (1)	*Column (2)*
Meteorological Office Station	*Specified Alternative Station*
Meteorological Office Station	Specified Alternative Station
Aberporth	Pembrey Sands
Albemarle	Redesdale Camp
Bingley, No 2	Stonyhurst
Boscombe Down	Westonbirt
Braemar No 2	Aboyne No 2
Capel Curig No 3	Lake Vyrnwy No 2
Cardinham, Bodmin	North Wyke
Carlisle	Keswick
Charlwood	Kenley Airfield
Coleshill	Pershore College
Crosby	Rhyl No 2
Culdrose	Scilly: St. Marys Airport
Dunstaffnage	Skye: Lusa
Edinburgh, Gogarbank	Strathallan Airfield
Eskdalemuir	Redesdale Camp
Gravesend, Broadness	Kenley Airfield
Hawarden Airport	Crosby
Heathrow	Gravesend, Broadness
Hereford, Credenhill	Pershore College
High Wycombe, HQ Air	Rothamsted
Hurn	Swanage
Keele	Shawbury
Kinloss	Lossiemouth
Lake Vyrnwy No 2	Shawbury
Langdon Bay	Gravesend, Broadness

Column (1) *Meteorological Office Station*	Column (2) *Specified Alternative Station*
Leconfield	Linton on Ouse
Linton on Ouse	Bramham
Liscombe	North Wyke
Llysdinam	Sennybridge No 2
Mona	Rhyl No 2
North Wyke	Okehampton, East Okement Farm
Redesdale Camp	Albemarle
Rhyl No 2	Crosby
Rochdale	Rostherne No 2
St. Athan	Mumbles Head
St. Bees Head No 2	Threave
Shap	Keswick
Sheffield	Nottingham, Watnall
Stonyhurst	Bingley, No 2
Thorney Island	Hurn
Threave	Dundrennan
Tiree	Skye: Lusa
Trawsgoed	Llysdinam
Tredegar, Bryn Bach Park No 2	Sennybridge No 2
Tulloch Bridge	Aviemore]

p.1492, *amendment to the Social Fund Winter Fuel Payment Regulations 2000 (SI 2000/729) reg.2(1)(a)(ii) (Social Fund winter fuel payments)*

With effect from September 21, 2015, reg.2(1) and (2) of the Social Fund Winter Fuel Payment (Amendment) Regulations 2014 amended reg.2(1)(a)(ii) by substituting the words "any of the countries listed in the Schedule to these Regulations" for the words "Switzerland or an EEA state other than the United Kingdom".   **3.039**

p.1494, *annotation to the Social Fund Winter Fuel Payment Regulations 2000 (SI 2000/729) reg.2 (Social Fund winter fuel payments)*

Replace the first two paragraphs in item (a) of the commentary with the following paragraphs: **3.040** "(a) He or she is either ordinarily resident in Great Britain, or in one of the countries listed in the Schedule to the Regulations, in the qualifying week (i.e. the week commencing on the third Monday in September (see reg.1(2)).

Claimants who qualify on the basis of habitual residence in a scheduled country must also fall within the personal scope of (EEC) or of Regulation (EC) 883/2004 and have a "genuine and sufficient link to the United Kingdom social security system": see para.(4) and the commentary on Regulation (EC) 883/2004 in Vol.III."

p.1499, *amendment to the Social Fund Winter Fuel Payment Regulations 2000 (SI 2000/729), insertion of new Schedule (Countries)*

3.041   With effect from September 21, 2015, reg.2(1) and (2) of the Social Fund Winter Fuel Payment (Amendment) Regulations 2014 amended reg.2(1)(a)(ii) by inserting the following Schedule at the end of the Regulations:

"**Regulation 2**

SCHEDULE

Countries
Republic of Austria
Kingdom of Belgium
Republic of Bulgaria
Republic of Croatia
Czech Republic
Kingdom of Denmark
Republic of Estonia
Republic of Finland
Federal Republic of Germany
Republic of Hungary
Republic of Iceland
Republic of Ireland
Republic of Italy
Republic of Latvia
Principality of Liechtenstein
Swiss Confederation."
Republic of Lithuania

Countries
Grand Duchy of Luxembourg
Kingdom of the Netherlands
Kingdom of Norway
Republic of Poland
Republic of Romania
Slovak Republic
Republic of Slovenia
Kingdom of Sweden
Swiss Confederation."

pp.1536–1537, *annotation to the Social Fund Maternity and Funeral Expenses (General) Regulations 2005 (SI 2005/3061) reg.10(1)(a) (Deductions from an award of a funeral payment)*

Para.(1)(a) of reg.10 (which provides that the amount of any assets of the deceased which are available to the responsible person without a formal grant of representation "shall be deducted from the amount of any . . . funeral payment which would otherwise be payable") was considered by the Upper Tribunal in *TG v SSWP (SF)* [2015] UKUT 0571 (AAC). In that case, the claimant made an internet transfer of £2,500 from his late mother's bank account to his own shortly before his mother died on a Sunday afternoon. However, as Sunday was not a business day, the deceased's bank statements did not show the money leaving her account until the following day. Whether or not, the claimant was entitled to a funeral payment depended upon whether the sum of £2,500 was an asset of the deceased at the time of her death. **3.042**

Judge Rowley accepted the Secretary of State's submission in support of the appeal that " . . . where a transfer is ordered prior to death, notwithstanding that the transaction does not clear until after the death, the funds which are the subject of the transfer are, generally speaking, no longer "assets of the deceased" available to the responsible person". That proposition was subject to any contrary provision in the contractual arrangements between the deceased and her bank. However, there was no such provision in *TG*. Rather, the evidence from the bank was that when one of its customers transferred funds using internet banking the funds would be applied to the payee's account within minutes even if the transfer were made on a non-business day, and even though, in those circumstances, the payment would only show on the customer's statement as being paid on the next following business day.

The claimant said that his mother had owed him the money and that he had made the transfer on her instructions. However, the First-tier Tribunal did not accept that the transfer represented a genuine reimbursement of money owed to the claimant. Rather, it viewed the transaction as a means of reducing the mother's estate prior to her death. Judge Rowley held that the motivation behind the transfer was irrelevant. The question to be determined was whether there were assets of the deceased that were available to the responsible person. If the transfer was validly made, then the transferred assets did not fall within reg.10(1)(a).

p.1573, *annotation to s.6K of the new style Jobseekers Act 1995 (Sanction for failure to comply with a work-related requirement)*

3.043   See *SA v SSWP (JSA)* [2015] UKUT 454 (AAC), discussed in the entry for p.116, for what might or might not amount to a failure to comply with a work preparation requirement.

p.1598, *amendment to the Jobseeker's Allowance Regulations 2013 (SI 2013/378), reg.2(2) (Definition of "training allowance")*

3.044   With effect from May 26, 2015, art.25 of Sch.3 to the Deregulation Act 2015 (Consequential Amendments) Order 2015 (SI 2015/971) amended para.(a) of the definition of "training allowance" in reg.2(2) by omitting ", the Chief Executive of Skills Funding".

p.1647, *amendment to the Jobseeker's Allowance Regulations 2013 (SI 2013/378), reg.42(3) and (4) (Remunerative work: hours that count)*

3.045   With effect from April 8, 2013, art.7 and para.52 of Sch. to the Armed Forces and Reserve Forces Compensation Scheme (Consequential Provisions: Subordinate Legislation) Order 2013 (SI 2013/591) amended paras (3) and (4) of reg.42 as follows. In para.(3)(c)(i), "or" after "care component" is omitted and "or armed forces independence payment" is inserted after "daily living component". In para.(3)(c)(ii), "armed forces independence payment," is inserted after "attendance allowance,". In para.(3)(c)(iv) "armed forces independence payment," is inserted after "attendance allowance," in both places. In para.(4), the following definition is added before the definition of "disability living allowance":

> ""armed forces independence payment" means armed forces independence payment under the Armed Forces and Reserve Forces (Compensation Scheme) Order 2011;"

These amendments were omitted in error from the 2015/16 and earlier editions of the main volume.

PART IV

UPDATING MATERIAL
VOLUME III

ADMINISTRATION, ADJUDICATION AND
THE EUROPEAN DIMENSION

Commentary by

Mark Rowland

Robin White

p.xvii, *Using this Book—Northern Ireland legislation*

As mentioned in the main volume, the Welfare Reform and Work Bill that was intended to replicate in Northern Ireland most of the provisions of the Welfare Reform Act 2012 failed to pass its final stage in the Northern Ireland Assembly in May 2015 because it had not gained the necessary cross-community support. This had substantial budgetary implications because the United Kingdom Government funds welfare in Northern Ireland only up to the levels that apply in Great Britain and the 2012 Act had achieved a substantial reduction of expenditure in Great Britain. In consequence, there were 11 weeks of talks between the United Kingdom Government, Northern Ireland politicians and the Irish Government (under the approach required by the 1998 Belfast Agreement), leading to an agreement on November 17, 2015 which resulted in the Northern Ireland (Welfare Reform) Act 2015 being passed by the United Kingdom Parliament and receiving Royal Assent on November 25, 2015. It is a short statute, authorising the making of Orders in Council to make provision in connection with social security in Northern Ireland, provided that any such Order in Council is made by the end of 2016. The Welfare Reform (Northern Ireland) Order 2015 (SI 2015/2006) was duly made on December 9, 2015 and, by virtue of s.2 of the Act, is treated as an Act of the Northern Ireland Assembly. It is similar to the Bill that had failed in the Assembly seven months earlier. Most of the provisions in it will come into force in accordance with commencement orders made by the Department for Social Development. Northern Ireland legislation will then converge again with Great Britain legislation and, for instance, personal independence payment will be introduced in Northern Ireland.

pp.6–7, *annotation to the Forfeiture Act 1982 s.4 (Upper Tribunal to decide whether forfeiture rule applies to social security benefits)*

In *Henderson v Wilcox* [2015] EWHC 3469 (Ch), the High Court considered whether to modify the forfeiture rule under s.2 insofar as it affected the passing of property under a will and decided not to modify it in a case where, although a hospital order had been made under s.37 of the Mental Health Act 2013, the beneficiary under the will had been convicted of the manslaughter of his mother on the basis of an absence of intention to kill or cause serious injury, rather than on the ground of diminished responsibility,. The assault had been a serious one and the culmination of a series of attacks for at least several months and, although the assailant had had a low IQ and had been frustrated by having to assume the role of carer of his mother in circumstances where he did not have the necessary life skills, he had had a good understanding of what he was doing and that it was wrong. The judge said: "Sympathy for the applicant is not . . . the guiding factor for the court. . . . I must be satisfied that justice requires modification of the forfeiture rule."   4.000.1

Although the term "relevant enactment" as defined in subs.(5) includes war pensions schemes made under the first three statutes mentioned in the definition, it does not include the main war pensions scheme covering former members of the Armed Forces injured or killed due to service before 6 April 2005, which is not made under those enactments. This is presumably because that scheme contains its own, rather broader, forfeiture provision in respect of which decisions are made by the Secretary of State for Defence with a right of appeal to the First-tier Tribunal (War Pensions and Armed Forces Compensation Chamber) in England and Wales or a Pensions Appeal Tribunal in Scotland or Northern Ireland. The war pensions schemes to which the 1982 Act applies are the scheme covering civilians injured by enemy action in the Second World War, various schemes covering merchant seaman and other civilians who served afloat in that conflict and the scheme covering members of the Polish Armed Forces who served under British command, none of which schemes has a forfeiture provision. On the other hand, the Armed Forces Compensation Scheme that applies in respect of members of the Armed Forces injured or killed due to service since April 2005 is a "relevant enactment" for the purposes of the 1982 Act because it is made under s.1 of the Armed Forces (Pensions and Compensation) Act 2004.

p.55, *annotation* to *Social Security Administration Act 1992 s.71 (Overpayments—general)*

AH, VH and MH v SSWP (DLA) [2015] UKUT 108 (AAC) is reported as [2015] AACR 40.

4.001   In *JF v SSWP (DLA)* [2015] UKUT 267 (AAC) and *AF v SSWP (DLA)* [2015] UKUT 266, Judge Wikeley sets out the due process requirements that apply in overpayment cases where the claimant's credibility is in issue. Care must be taken to consider all the evidence, to show why a discretion to consider an issue not raised in this appeal was exercised, to make clear findings of fact which reflect all the evidence before it, and to be very careful about considering even part of the evidence in the absence of the claimant (part of a DVD was viewed by the tribunal while the claimant was not in the room).

In *AS v SSWP (CA)* [2015] UKUT 592 (AAC) Judge Wright deals with two issues: (a) what burden of proof falls on the Secretary of State where claimants state that they have made disclosure by way of telephone communication with the Department; and (b) how should a First-tier Tribunal deal with an established claim that there has not been judgment in a reasonable time, contrary to art.6 ECHR?

The issues arose in an overpayment case involving a claimed failure to disclose earnings on making a claim for carer's allowance where the existence of those earnings only came to light some years later. On the first question, the claimant's representative argued, relying on *CSB/ 347/1983* and *R(SB) 10/85*, that, in the face of the claimant's evidence that he had disclosed his earnings in a telephone call to the Department, the Secretary of State was required as a matter of law to adduce evidence as to the procedures in place at the relevant office of the Department at the relevant time, and could not merely adduce evidence that no record of the telephone conversation could be found. Judge Wright does not consider that *R(SB) 10/85* supports the proposition to be found in *CSB/*

347/1983. Furthermore, even if *CSB/347/1983* constituted a principle of law in December 1983 when it was decided, it did not survive the approach advocated in *Kerr v Department for Social Development* [2004] UKHL 23; *R 1/04(SF)* which explained that the inquisitorial approach adopted in tribunals meant that "it will rarely be necessary to resort to concepts taken from adversarial litigation such as the burden of proof" (para.63). Under s.12(8)(a) of the Social Security Act 1998 what evidence is or is not needed in any case will depend on the facts of the case. The circumstances of the case before Judge Wright did not put in issue the procedures for recording telephone conversations. Judge Wright concludes:

"43. Accordingly, in so far as the comments in *CSB/347/1983* about telephone recording systems was laying down a rule of law, in my judgment it should not longer be followed."

The second issue—that of delay—arose in the following circumstances. The Secretary of State made an entitlement decision on September 4, 2004 in respect of a non-entitlement to carer's allowance arising from April 16, 2001. But it was not until January 5, 2007 that an overpayment decision was made. There was then a five year delay before a letter dated April 11, 2007 was accepted as an appeal against the overpayment decision. The tribunal's decision was made in May 2014. In considering at paras 49–56 how the tribunal should have responded to this issue, Judge Wright assumes that the delays would amount to a failure to give judgment in a reasonable time in breach of Article 6 of the European Convention. It will usually be the case that a tribunal must proceed to determine the appeal notwithstanding the delay, and cannot simply not proceed on the grounds that there has been an unreasonable delay. The person affected must seek a remedy elsewhere in the form of compensation, and the tribunal has no power to award compensation: see *Cocchiarella v Italy* (App.64886/01) Judgment of Grand Chamber of March 29, 2006.

4.002

p.146, *amendment to Social Security Administration Act 1992 s.179 (Reciprocal agreements with countries outside the United Kingdom)*

With effect from July 7, 2015, s.23 and Sch.12 para.25 of the Pensions Act 2014 amended s.179 as follows:
    (a) by inserting the words ", Part 1 of the Pensions Act 2014" after the words "Part 4 of that Act";
    (b) by inserting the following after para.(ah) of subs.(4):

4.003

"(ai) to Part 1 of the Pensions Act 2014";

    (c) by inserting in subs.(5) the words "or Part 1 of the Pensions Act 2014" after the words "Act 2007";
    (d) by inserting the following after para.(ac) of subs.(5):

"(ad) state pension under Part 1 of the Pensions Act 2014;".

pp.185–187, *annotation to the Social Security (Recovery of Benefits) Act 1997 s.11 (Appeals against certificates of recoverable benefits)*

4.004   *Aviva Insurance Ltd v SSWP* [2015] UKUT 613 (AAC) was an appeal to the Upper Tribunal against a decision made on an appeal brought under s.11 of the 1997 Act as modified and applied to the recovery under the Social Security (Recovery of Benefits) (Lump Sum Payments) Regulations 2008 of lump sum payments made under the Pneumoconiosis etc. (Workers' Compensation) Act 1979. Having regard to *R(CR) 1/02* (mentioned in the main volume), it was accepted that the compensator was in principle entitled to argue that the payment made to the claimant under the 1979 Act ought not to have been made, although the argument was rejected on its merits.

pp.215–217, *annotation to the Social Security Act 1998 s.8(2) (Decisions by Secretary of State)*

4.005–6   *SSWP v HR (AA)* [2014] UKUT 571 (AAC) has been reported at [2015] AACR 26 and *SSWP v AK (AA)* [2015] UKUT 110 (AAC) has been reported at [2015] AACR 27.

pp.223–224, *annotation to the Social Security Act 1998 s.10(2) (Decisions superseding earlier decisions)*

4.007   In *MF v Redcar and Cleveland Borough Council (HB)* [2015] UKUT 634 (AAC), it is confirmed that a person may appeal against aspects of a decision superseding an earlier decision notwithstanding that the decision maker did not address his or her mind to those aspects of the decision on the supersession, having done so only when making the earlier decision.

pp.232–233, *annotation to the Social Security Act 1998 s.12(2) (The nature of an appeal to the First-tier Tribunal and the powers of the First-tier Tribunal)*

4.008   In *MF v Redcar and Cleveland Borough Council (HB)* [2015] UKUT 634 (AAC), the local authority had made a decision that included a reduction in the claimant's housing benefit on the ground of under-occupation and then superseded the decision solely on the ground of an increase in rent. It was held that the claimant was entitled to challenge the reduction in respect of under-occupation on an appeal against the supersession decision, albeit presumably only in respect of the period from the date the supersession decision took effect.

Even if delay in deciding a case is such as to breach an appellant's rights under art.6 of the European Convention on Human Rights, the First-tier Tribunal cannot provide a remedy on an appeal under s.12 of the 1998 Act (*AS v SSWP (CA)* [2015] UKUT 592 (AAC)).

pp.240–244, *annotation to the Social Security Act 1998, s.12(8)(a) (The First-tier Tribunal's power to consider an issue not raised by the appeal)*

The point made in *John v Information Commissioner* [2014] UKUT 444 (AAC) mentioned in the main volume—that a tribunal could prevent unfairness from arising by exercising its case-management powers where a party wished to take a new point—had already been made by the Court of Appeal in *Birkett v Department for the Environment, Food and Rural Affairs* [2011] EWCA Civ 1606, to which the Upper Tribunal referred.

4.008.1

p.253, *repeal of the Social Security Act 1998 s.15A(2) and (3) (Senior President of Tribunals' duty to report on adjudication standards of the Secretary of State)*

With effect from May 26, 2015, s.79 of the Deregulation Act 2015 repealed s.15A(2) and (3) of the 1998 Act. This particular duty to make an annual report to the Secretary of State (which was in practice delegated to the President of the Social Entitlement Chamber of the First-tier Tribunal) was a hang-over from the time when appeal tribunals were administered by the Secretary of State and the President of those appeal tribunals made the report. It could be regarded as anomalous under the new tribunals system. Comments on the Secretary of State's adjudication standards can still be made, but there is no longer a duty to make an annual report and, perhaps more importantly, there is no longer any duty on anyone to publish any comments.

4.009

pp.259–260, *annotation to the Social Security Act 1998 s.19 (Medical examination required by the Secretary of State)*

Section 19(1) is in permissive terms and does not require that a person be referred to a health care professional for examination and report. Therefore, the Secretary of State is entitled to, and should, consider whether an examination is really necessary in a case where a claimant has contended that (e.g., for mental health reasons) he or she has good cause for not attending any examination. If the Secretary of State is satisfied that the claimant cannot reasonably be expected to attend for an examination but also considers that there is insufficient evidence upon which to make a decision awarding benefit, it may be appropriate for him to make a decision not to award the benefit. However, there may be adequate written evidence to justify an award. Where the First-tier Tribunal allows an appeal against a decision made under subs.(3), it has the power to give a substantive decision on the claimant's entitlement to benefit but it will rarely be able to do so without adjourning either for an examination or to give the Secretary of State an opportunity to make further submissions. It cannot direct the healthcare professional to carry out a domiciliary visit for the purpose of a medical examination under this section, but it can make a suggestion to that effect. (It can direct a domiciliary visit when exercising its own power to refer a case to a health care professional under s.20(2).) See *CG v SSWP (II)* [2015] UKUT 400 (AAC).

4.010

p.393, *annotation to the Social Security (Claims and Payments) Regulations 1987 (SI 1987/1968) reg.6 (Date of claim)*

4.010.1   The annotation to reg.6(22) notes that the Department had advised CPAG that the regulations would be amended to include personal independence payment as a "relevant benefit", but the Department has subsequently advised that is now has no current plans to amend the regulations to this effect.

p.431, *annotation to the Social Security (Claims and Payments) Regulations 1987 (SI 1987/1968) reg.19 (Time for claiming benefit)*

4.011   In *SSWP v PG (JSA)* [2015] UKUT 616 (AAC) Judge Wright disagrees with Judge Wikeley's conclusions in *SK-G v SSWP (JSA)* [2014] UKUT 430 that information on the Department's website does not constitute information given by an officer of the Department within reg.19(5)(d). Judge Wright had the benefit of argument in an oral hearing and provides detailed consideration of the process by which information finds its way onto the Department's website (paras 18–20)—in this case the *DirectGov* website. Judge Wright concludes that information on the website is capable of falling within the scope of reg.19(5)(d).

pp.629-633, *annotation to the Social Security and Child Support (Decisions and Appeals) Regulations 1999 (SI 1999/991) reg.6(2)(g) and (r) (Supersession of decisions)*

4.012   In *FN v SSWP (ESA)* [2015] UKUT 670 (AAC), a three-judge panel has broadly agreed with *JC v DSD (IB)* [2011] NICom 177; [2014] AACR 30 and also both *ST v SSWP (ESA)* [2012] UKUT 469 (AAC) and *AM v SSWP (ESA)* [2013] UKUT 458 (AAC) (all mentioned in the main volume and concerned with the relevance of the reports of previous medical examinations) but has stressed that the previous adjudication history and associated evidence is not always relevant and that, even if the Secretary of State has not produced all the information and evidence that he should have produced with his response to an appeal, it does not necessarily follow that the First-tier Tribunal's decision will be wrong in law and liable to be set aside. See further the supplementary annotation to r.24 of the Tribunal Procedure (First-tier Tribunal) (Social Entitlement Chamber) Rules 2008, below.

The three-judge panel also expressed agreement with *CIB/1509/2004* (also mentioned in the main volume) and, in particular, with the Commissioner's statement that reg.6(2)(g) merely authorised a supersession but did not determine the outcome. It confirmed the conventional view of the way that reg.6(2)(g) and (r) operates, saying—

> "70. . . . although we are not asked to consider the practical application of regulation 6(2)(g) or 6(2)(r)(i), we re-emphasise that the purpose of both provisions is to provide that the obtaining of a medical report or medical evidence following an examination is in itself a

ground for supersession and that, accordingly, there is no longer a requirement to identify a regulation 6(2)(a)(i) change of circumstances in order to supersede an IB or ESA decision."

pp.671–672, *annotation to the Social Security and Child Support (Decisions and Appeals) Regulations 1999 (SI 1999/991) reg.19 (Suspension and termination for failure to submit to medical examination)*

What was said in *CG v SSWP (II)* [2015] UKUT 400 (AAC) in the context of s.19 of the Social Security Act 1998 (see the supplementary annotation above) will apply equally to cases under reg.19 of the 1999 Regulations.   **4.013**

p.677, *annotation to the Social Security and Child Support (Decisions and Appeals) Regulations 1999 (SI 1999/991) reg.26 (Decisions against which an appeal lies)*

The second paragraph of this annotation (para.2.544 of the 2014–2015 edition of the main volume) was approved in *DT v SSWP (II)* [2015] UKUT 509 (AAC) at [56] insofar as it refers to the need for a new claim when a final assessment of disablement expires under the current legislation and to *R(I) 5/02* now being only of historical interest to the extent that it was concerned with the operation of s.47 of the Social Security Administration Act 1992.   **4.014**

p.938, *annotation to the Social Security (Recovery of Benefits) (Lump Sum Payments) Regulations 2008 Sch. (Modification of certain provisions of the Social Security (Recovery of Benefits) Act 1997)*

This Schedule applies, with modifications, a number of the provisions relating to adjudication in the 1997 Act to cases under the 2008 Regulations. In particular, ss.9 to 14 of the 1997 Act, relating to reviews and appeals, are applied as modified. In *Aviva Insurance Ltd v SSWP* [2015] UKUT 613 (AAC), it was accepted that, having regard to *R(CR) 1/02*, a compensator was in principle entitled to argue on an appeal to the First-tier Tribunal that the payment made to the claimant under the Pneumoconiosis etc. (Workers' Compensation) Act 1979 that the Secretary of State now sought to recover ought not to have been made because the Secretary of State had misconstrued the 1979 Act when awarding the payment. However, the argument advanced by the compensator was rejected on its merits.   **4.015**

p.1039, *annotation to art.20 TFEU*

The second and third questions referred by the Court of Appeal in *Secretary of State for the Home Department v NA* (C-115/15) [2015] OJ C171/20 are: **4.016**

"2. Does an EU citizen have an EU law right to reside in a host member state under Articles 20 and 21 of the TFEU in circumstances where the only state within the EU in which the citizen is entitled to reside is his state of nationality, but there is a finding of fact by a competent tribunal that the removal of the citizen from the host member state to his state of nationality would breach his rights under Article 8 of the ECHR or Article 7 of the Charter of Fundamental Rights of the EU?

3. If the EU citizen in (2) (above) is a child, does the parent having sole care of that child have a derived right of residence in the host member state if the child would have to accompany the parent on removal of the parent from the host member state?"

p.1044, *annotation to art.21 TFEU*

4.017   In Case C-308/14, on October 6, 2015, Advocate General Cruz Villalón expressed the opinion that the challenged United Kingdom legislation did not breach European Union law. He said,

"99. In conclusion, I consider that it does not constitute discrimination prohibited by Article 4 of Regulation 883/2004 if national legislation provides that, when examining claims for social benefits such as child benefit or child tax credit, the Member State's authorities may carry out the checks necessary to ensure that nationals of other Member States claiming those benefits are lawfully resident in its territory. However, for that purpose, the authorities responsible for carrying out those checks will, in any case, from a procedural point of view, have to observe the principles described above, in particular, the principle of proportionality, as well as the provisions of the second paragraph of Article 14(2), Article 15(1), and Article 30 and 31 of Directive 2004/38."

The Court will issue its judgment in the case in due course.

p.1062, *annotation to art.49 TFEU*

4.018   *SSWP v HH (SPC)* [2015] UKUT 583 (AAC) is an example of when self-employment will be regarded as not genuine and effective economic activity, but rather purely marginal and ancillary activity which does not qualify the claimant to be regarded as a self-employed person under art.49.

p.1094, *annotation to Regulation (EU) 492/2011 art.10*

4.019   The fourth question referred by the Court of Appeal in *Secretary of State for the Home Department v NA* (C-115/15) [2015] OJ C171/20 is:

"4. Does a child have a right to reside in the host Member State pursuant to Article 12 of Regulation (EEC) No 1612/68/EEC (now Article 10 of Regulation 492/2011/EU) if the child's Union citizen parent, who has been employed in the host Member State, has ceased to reside in the host Member State before the child enters education in that state?"

p.1108, *annotation to Directive 2004/38/EC art.3 (beneficiaries)*

For some observations on the application of the principle established 4.020
in *Surinder Singh (C-370/90)* [1992] ECR I-4265 to the rights set out in
art.3(2), see *JS v DSD (JSA)* [2015] NICom 53.

p.1114, *annotation to Directive 2004/38/EC art.7 (right of residence for
more than three months)*

The judgment of the Court of Justice of June 19, 2014 in *Jessy Saint-* 4.021
Prix v SSWP (C-507/12) [2015] 1 CMLR 5 left open a number of
questions about how the new approach to entitlement to benefit during
a maternity period would operate. The most significant of those questions have been answered in *SSWP v SFF; ADR v SSWP; and CS v
London Borough of Barnet and SSWP* [2015] UKUT 502 (AAC). Judge
Ward comes to the following conclusions on what he labels "the Saint-
Prix right":
   (a) The right is to be assessed prospectively, since, for the right to be
       effective, a woman will need a decision at the time of her claim,
       and not once she has subsequently returned to work or to seeking
       work (paras 20–24).
   (b) The right is available to those who are workers by virtue of
       actually having been in employment and to those who are no
       longer working but who retain the right to be treated as a worker.
       Judge Ward leaves open the question of whether a person who is
       a worker within art.45 TFEU solely by reason of being a work
       seeker enjoys the right (para.25).
   (c) The start of the right is determined on the facts of each case, but
       in practice this will generally be the start of the eleven weeks prior
       to the expected date of confinement (para.26).
   (d) The duration of the right will also be determined by the facts of
       each case which must be viewed in the context of the 52 week
       period of ordinary maternity leave and additional maternity leave
       combined (paras 27–37).
   (e) Obviously an actual return to work in some form will suffice, but
       it will also suffice if the woman returns to seeking work where the
       conditions of art.7(3)(b) or (c) of the Citizenship Directive are
       complied with (paras 38–43).
   (f) The period during which a woman enjoys the right contributes to
       the period of time necessary to acquire a permanent right of
       residence under art.16 of the Citizenship Directive (para.44).
The judgment of September 15, 2015 in the *Alimanovic case* (C-67/14)
requires some reconsideration of the scope of the Court's judgment in
the *Brey case* (C-140/12), and certainly places much less emphasis on
rights flowing from citizenship of the Union than the Court had done on
the *Dano case* (C-333/13) where the Court had repeated its mantra that
citizenship of the Union is a "fundamental status" leading to a requirement for equal treatment.
The *Alimanovic case* concerned entitlements flowing solely from hold- 4.022
ing the status of being a work seeker. Under German legislation, the

claimants were refused a subsistence benefit (which the Court characterized as "social assistance") following their loss of retained worked status under art.7(3)(c) of the Citizenship Directive. The claimants' status was solely that of work seekers. The Court re-affirms its decision in the *Dano case* that Union citizens can only claim social assistance on the basis of art.24(2) of the Citizenship Directive when their residence meets the conditions set out in the Directive. Recalling its decision in *Vatsouras and Koupatantze* (C-22/08 and C-23/08), the Court notes the entitlement to social assistance during the six month period during which worker status is retained under art.7(3)(c) and the possibility that a right to residence as work seekers might arise on the ending of the period of retained worker status. However, the derogation in art.24(2) permits Member States to refuse social assistance where claimants' right of residence falls within art.14(4)(b). Those in this situation would, following the *Brey case*, seem to be entitled to an individual assessment of their circumstances, but the Court says:—

> "59. . . . , although the Court has held that Directive 2004/38 requires a Member State to take account of the individual situation of the person concerned before it adopts an expulsion measure or finds that the residence of that person is placing an unreasonable burden on its social assistance system (judgment in *Brey* . . .), no such individual assessment is necessary in circumstances such as those at issue in the main proceedings.
>
> 60. Directive 2004/38, establishing a gradual system as regards the retention of the status of 'worker' which seeks to safeguard the right of residence and access to social assistance, itself takes into consideration various factors characterising the individual situation of each applicant for social assistance, and, in particular, the duration of the exercise of any economic activity."

It followed that the German legislation was not in breach of the requirements of the Citizenship Directive.

The effect of the judgment in the *Alimanovic case* on the judgment in the *Brey case* is far from clear. The two judgments can only stand side by side if the obligation arising under art.7(1)(b) for an individual assessment of whether a claimant is an unreasonable burden on the social assistance of the host Member State can somehow be decoupled from the consideration of entitlement to social assistance for those falling within art.14(4)(b). That seems an exceedingly subtle distinction.

p.1129, *annotation to Directive 2004/38/EC art.13 (Retention of the right of residence by family members in the event of divorce, annulment of marriage or termination of registered partnership)*

4.023   The first of four questions referred to the Court of Justice by the Court of Appeal in *Secretary of State for the Home Department v NA* (C-115/15) [2015] OJ C171/20 is:

> "Must a third country national ex-spouse of a Union citizen be able to show that their former spouse was exercising Treaty rights in the host

Member state at the time of their divorce in order to retain a right of residence under Article 13(2) of Directive 2004/38/EC?"

p.1131, *annotation to Directive 2004/38/EC art.24 (General rule for Union citizens and their family members)*

In *Secretary of State for the Home Department v Jovita Ojo* [2015]   4.023.1
EWCA Civ 1301, the Court of Appeal ruled:

"20. In my view none of the authorities to which we were referred supports the proposition that the court can treat the period during which Mrs Ojo ceased to be dependent on her mother as analogous to a period of absence from the United Kingdom. The acquisition of a permanent right of residence depends on continuous residence in a qualifying status and the Directive makes no provision for changes in status of the kind which occurred in this case, nor is there any reason why it should so so. There is a distinction to be drawn between residence and status which makes it inapposite to draw an analogy between the two."

p.1135, *annotation to Directive 2004/38/EC art.17 (Exemptions for persons no longer working in the host Member State and their family members)*

TG v SSWP [2015] UKUT 50 (AAC) is under appeal to the Court of   4.024
appeal.

p.1139, *annotation to Directive 2004/38/EC art.24 (Equal treatment)*

Note the judgment of the Grand Chamber of the Court of Justice in   4.025
the *Alimanovic case* (C-67/14) discussed above in the update to the
annotations to art.7 of the Citizenship Directive.

p.1166, *annotation to Regulation (EC) 883/2004 art.3 (Matters covered)*

Commission v Slovak Republic (C-433/13) concerned a complaint by   4.026
the Commission that Slovak Republic breached the requirements of arts
7 and 21 of Regulation 883/2004 in refusing the export of the care
allowance and allied benefits. However, the Court concluded that,
because the Member State retained a discretion over the award of the
benefit even where the conditions of entitlement were met that the
benefit did "not constitute social security benefits within the meaning of
Regulation No 883/2004" (para.83).

p.1170, *annotation to Regulation (EC) 883/2004 art.4 (Equality of treatment)*

In Case C-308/14, on October 6, 2015, Advocate General Cruz   4.027
Villalón expressed the opinion that the challenged United Kingdom
legislation did not breach European Union law. He said,

"99. In conclusion, I consider that it does not constitute discrimination prohibited by Article 4 of Regulation 883/2004 if national legislation provides that, when examining claims for social benefits such as child benefit or child tax credit, the Member State's authorities may carry out the checks necessary to ensure that nationals of other Member States claiming those benefits are lawfully resident in its territory. However, for that purpose, the authorities responsible for carrying out those checks will, in any case, from a procedural point of view, have to observe the principles described above, in particular, the principle of proportionality, as well as the provisions of the second paragraph of Article 14(2), Article 15(1), and Article 30 and 31 of Directive 2004/38."

The Court will issue its judgment in the case in due course.

p.1175, *annotation to Regulation (EC) 883/2004 art.7 (Waiving of residence rules)*

4.028 The Supreme Court in *SSWP v Tolley (deceased, acting by her personal representative)* [2015] UKSC 55 has referred the following questions to the Court of Justice:

"1. Is the care component of the United Kingdom's Disability Living Allowance properly classified as an invalidity rather than a cash sickness benefit for the purpose of Regulation No 1408/71?

2.(i) Does a person who ceases to be entitled to UK Disability Living Allowance as a matter of UK domestic law, because she has moved to live in another member state, and who has ceased all occupational activity before such move, but remains insured against old age under the UK social security system, cease to be subject to the legislation of the UK for the purpose of article 13(2)(f) of Regulation No 1408/71?

(ii) Does such a person in any event remain subject to the legislation of the UK in the light of Point 19(c) of the United Kingdom's annex VI to the Regulation?

(iii) If she has ceased to be subject to the legislation of the UK within the meaning of article 13(2)(f), is the UK obliged or merely permitted by virtue of Point 20 of annex VI to apply the provisions of Chapter 1 of Title III to the Regulation to her?

3. (i) Does the broad definition of an employed person in *Dodl* apply for the purposes of articles 19 to 22 of the Regulation, where the person has ceased all occupational activity before moving to another member state, notwithstanding the distinction drawn in Chapter 1 of Title III between, on the one hand, employed and self-employed persons and, on the other hand, unemployed persons?

(ii) If it does apply, is such a person entitled to export the benefit by virtue of either article 9 or article 22? Does article 22(1)(b) operate to prevent a claimant's entitlement to the care component of DLA being defeated by a residence requirement imposed by national legislation on a transfer of residence to another member state?"

The Court of Justice has registered the case as Case C-430/15: [2015] OJ C320/23

p.1179, *annotation to Regulation (EC) 883/2004 art.11 (General rules)*

SSWP v AK (AA) [2015] UKUT 110 (AAC) is reported as [2015] AACR 27. 4.029

p.1189, *general note to Chapter 1 (sickness, maternity and equivalent paternity benefits*

The Department has issued two memos concerning the award of sickness benefits: Memo DMG 26/15 *Deciding the competent State to pay cash sickness benefits*, and Memo DMG 27/15 *Action to take once competency has been decided.* Both memos are dated November 2015. 4.029.1

p.1229, *annotation to Chapter 8 (Family benefits)*

In *BM v HMRC* [2015] UKUT 526 Judge Jacobs draws attention to incorrect submissions in a number of appeals asserting that the provisions in Regulation 883/2004 on family benefits are the same as those in the predecessor Regulation 1408/71, when that is patently not the case. Tribunals should note that the provisions of Regulation 883/2004 on family benefits are significantly different from the provisions in the earlier regulation. 4.030

p.1230, *annotation to Regulation (EC) 883/2004 art.67 (Members of a family residing in another Member State)*

The *Trapkowski case* (C-378/14) judgment of October 22, 2015, concerned the interpretation of art.60 of Regulation 987/2009 which sets out the procedure for applying arts 67 and 68 of Regulation 883/2004. The father was resident in Germany and was divorced from the mother who lived in Poland with their son. In August 2012 the father claimed family benefits for the son; he had been at various times in work and in receipt of unemployment benefits. At the date of claim, he was in receipt of unemployment benefit. Meanwhile, the mother was at the material time in paid employment in Poland, but had not claimed family benefits there (or in Germany). The German authorities refused the father's claim on the grounds that it was principally the mother who was entitled to family benefit under German law. In response to the first question referred by the national court, the Court of Justice ruled:— 4.031

"38. It is apparent from a combined reading of Article 67 of Regulation No 883/2004 and Article 60(1) of Regulation No 987/2009, first, that a person may claim family benefits for members of his family who reside in a Member State other than that responsible for paying those benefits and, second, that the possibility to apply for family benefits is granted not only to persons who reside in the Member State required to pay the family benefits, but also to all the 'persons concerned', who may claim those benefits, including the parents of the child for whom the benefits are claimed.

39. Accordingly, given that the parents of the child for whom family benefits are claimed fall within the definition of 'persons concerned' within the meaning of Article 60(1) of Regulation No 987/2009, authorised to claim payment of those benefits, it is conceivable that a parent who resides in a Member State other than that required to pay those benefits is the person entitled to receive those benefits, if all the other conditions laid down by national law are also met.

40. It is for the competent national authority to determine the persons who, in accordance with national law, have a right to family benefits."

4.032   In response to the second question referred, the Court said:—

"42. By its second question, the referring court asks essentially whether Article 60(1), third sentence, of Regulation No 987/2009 must be interpreted as meaning that the parent of the child for whom family benefits are paid, who resides in the Member State required to pay those benefits, must be granted entitlement to those benefits because the other parent, who resides in another Member State, has not made an application for family benefits.

43. To answer that question, it should be recalled, as a preliminary point, that Regulations No 987/2009 and No 883/2004 do not determine the persons entitled to family benefits, even though they lay down the rules which enable the persons entitled to claim those benefits to be determined.

44. The persons entitled to family benefits are, as is clear from Article 67 of Regulation No 883/200, to be determined in accordance with national law.

45. Furthermore, it must be observed that Article 60(1), third sentence, of Regulation No 987/2009 provides that where a person entitled to claim the benefits does not exercise his right, the competent institutions of the Member States must take into account such applications made by the persons or institutions mentioned in that provision which include the 'other parent'.

46. First, it appears both from the wording and the general scheme of Article 60(1) of Regulation No 987/2009 that a distinction must be made between making a claim for family benefits and the right to receive such benefits.

47. Second, it is also clear from the wording of that article that it is sufficient if one of the persons able to claim the benefit of those family benefits makes an application for such benefits, so that the competent institution of the Member State must take that application into consideration.

48. However, EU law does not preclude such an institution, by applying national law, from finding that the person entitled to receive child benefits is a person other than the person who made the application for those benefits.

49. Therefore, where all the conditions for the grant of child benefits have been met and those benefits are actually granted, the issue as

to which parent is regarded under national law as the person entitled to receive such benefits is irrelevant (see, to that effect, judgment in *Hoever and Zachow*, C-245/94 and C-312/94, . . . , paragraph 37)."

p.1234, *annotation to Regulation (EC) 883/2004 art.70 (General provisions)*

GS v SSWP (DLA) [2015] UKUT 687 (AAC) decides that the "age 65 cut off" in the DLA scheme does not breach EU law.   **4.032.1**

p.1247, *annotation to Regulation (EC) 883/2004 art.81 (Claims, declarations or appeals)*

SSWP v AK (AA) [2015] UKUT 110 (AAC) is reported as [2015] AACR 27.   **4.033**

p.1308, *annotation to Regulation (EC) 987/2009 art.3 (Scope and rules for exchanges between the persons concerned and institutions)*

SSWP v HR (AA) [2014] UKUT 571 (AAC) is reported as [2015] AACR 26.   **4.034**

p.1310, *annotation to Regulation (EC) 987/2009 art.6 (Provisional application of legislation and provisional granting of benefits)*

SSWP v HR (AA) [2014] UKUT 571 (AAC) is reported as [2015] AACR 26; and *SSWP v AK (AA)* [2015] UKUT 110 (AAC) is reported as [2015] AACR 27.   **4.035**

p.1334, *annotation to Regulation (EC) No 987/2009 art.60 (Procedure for applying Articles 67 and 68 of the basic Regulation)*

See the judgment of the Court of Justice of October 22, 2015 in the *Trapkowski case* (C-378/14) discussed in the update to the annotations to art.67 of Regulation 883/2004 (p.1230 above).   **4.036**

p.1385, *annotation to Council Directive 79/7/EEC, art.4*

The Supreme Court has given permission to appeal against the judgment of the Court of Appeal in *MB v SSWP* [2014] EWCA Civ 1112.   **4.037**

p.1445, *annotation to Human Rights Act 1998 Sch.1 art.8 ECHR (Right to respect for private and family life)*

Cameron Mathieson, a deceased child (by his father Craig Mathieson) v SSWP [2015] UKSC 47 is also reported as [2015] AACR 44.   **4.038**

p.1448, *annotation to Human Rights Act 1998 Sch.1 art.14 ECHR (Prohibition of discrimination)*

Cameron Mathieson, a deceased child (by his father Craig Mathieson) v SSWP [2015] UKSC 47 is also reported as [2015] AACR 44.   **4.039**

p.1448, *annotation to Human Rights Act 1998 Sch.1 art.14 (Prohibition of discrimination)*

4.040   *R. (on the application of Rutherford and others) v Secretary of State for Work and Pensions* [2016] EWCA Civ 29 rules that the different treatment for children, with regard to the bedroom tax rules, constitutes discriminatory treatment which is manifestly without reasonable foundation contrary to art.14. The judgment is under appeal to the Supreme Court, where it is to be listed to be heard alongside *R (on the application of MA and others) v Secretary of State for Work and Pensions.* The Court of Appeal judgment in that case is at [2014] EWCA Civ 13.

4.041   In *JH v HMRC (CHB)* [2015] UKUT 479 (AAC), Judge Levenson disapplied the provisions of reg.3(3) of the Child Benefit (General) Regulations 2006 as being in breach of art.14 when read with art.1 of Protocol 1 in a case involving the refusal of child benefit in respect of an 18 year old on the autistic spectrum ("the young person") who was being educated at home under arrangements funder by the local authority. The preclusion of benefit in such cases where the home schooling had not started before the young person was 16 years of age amounted to a difference of treatment which required justification if it was not to be unlawful discrimination. No justification was found for the difference in treatment in relation to the age when home schooling started, and this was accepted by HMRC.

pp.1473–1478, *annotation to the Tribunals, Courts and Enforcement Act 2007 s.3(1) (The First-tier Tribunal)*

4.042   In *R. (Ingenious Media Holdings plc) v Revenue and Customs Commissioners* [2015] EWCA Civ 173; [2015] 1 W.L.R. 3183, the Court of Appeal made some useful comments on the relevance of Departmental guidance (although the Supreme Court has granted permission to appeal against the decision in that case). Sir Robin Jacob, with whom Tomlinson and Moore-Bick LJJ agreed, said of HMRC's *Information Disclosure Guide—*

"31. This was issued by HMRC mainly but not exclusively for the guidance of its officials. Substantial parts are nonetheless available to the public. However it is elementary that guides of this sort can have no binding effect on the proper construction of a statute. The law is made by Parliament, not pamphlets. Of course a guide by civil servants writing their interpretation of what the law means and how it would apply to particular cases, can in everyday practice be useful. But it is not definitive. It is like a commentary on a statute by an academic: it may be considered by a court as a view of what the statute may mean.

32. Such a Guide may even be useful as an aid in considering whether or not a government action was reasonable, should such a question arise. It may also be relevant in considering what might, in circumstances where the question arises, amount to a legitimate expectation as to how a government department may act. But such an

expectation has its limits: one cannot really have a legitimate expectation of the meaning of a statute from a pamphlet."

Nor, strictly speaking, can there be a legitimate expectation based on a policy of which the citizen is unaware. However, good administration requires that citizens be treated in accordance with a policy adopted by a Government department unless there are good reasons for not doing so and, in the absence of any reasons for departing from a policy, the courts will require conformity to it where it is favourable to the claimant. Accordingly, a respondent to an appeal to the First-tier Tribunal fails in his or her duty to draw relevant matters to the attention of the tribunal if no mention is made of the favourable policy in the response to the appeal (*Mandalia v Secretary of State for the Home Department* [2015] UKSC 59; [2015] 1 W.L.R. 4546).

Statements of fact in the Secretary of State's response to an appeal **4.043** may amount to evidence: see *AS v SSWP (CA)* [2015] UKUT 592 (AAC), in which it was said—
"The critical issue is what weight is to be attached to them, and that is for the First-tier Tribunal to assess. The blander or broader the statement, the less weight it might be given. However in this case there was a specific evidential statement made in the appeal response that a full search of the CA Unit's clerical records had been made and in my judgment that evidence was entitled to be given weight. The particular weight to be attached to it was a matter for the fact-finding tribunal to evaluate as part of its fact-finding jurisdiction, and does not here give rise to any error of law."

Although the claimant had said that he had telephoned the CA Unit and informed it of his employment and earnings, it was held that there was no rule of law requiring the Secretary of State to produce evidence as to his system for recording telephone conversations in order to show that the claimant had failed to disclose those material facts.

pp.1481–1484, *annotation to the Tribunals, Courts and Enforcement Act 2007 s.3(2) (Precedent in the Upper Tribunal)*

In *EC v SSWP (ESA)* [2015] UKUT 618 (AAC), a single judge of the **4.044** Upper Tribunal concluded that there were compelling reasons for disagreeing with a Tribunal of Social Security Commissioners in Northern Ireland on the ground that he had been provided by the Secretary of State with far more extra-statutory material that it was legitimate to take into account in construing the relevant legislation than the Northern Ireland Department for Social Development had provided to the Tribunal of Commissioners. Although the judge considered that he should treat a Tribunal of Commissioners in the same way as he would a three-judge panel of the Upper Tribunal, it seems doubtful that a single judge would generally feel entitled to disagree with a three-judge panel on such grounds. In *Dorset Healthcare NHS Foundation Trust v MH* [2009] UKUT 4 (AAC) (mentioned in the main volume), the only example of a compelling reason for a single judge not following a three-judge panel that is given is a decision of a superior court. No doubt a single judge may also decline to follow a decision of a three-judge panel that has overlooked other material that shows that its decision was unarguably wrong, but the position was not so clear cut in this case. However, the Chamber President had declined to convene a three-judge panel on the basis that, although the approach taken in the past suggested that a decision of a Tribunal of Commissioners should be treated in the same way as a decision of a three-judge panel of the Upper Tribunal, the Secretary of State's arguments should be put to a single judge and that "the place for removing problems flowing from divergent decisions" would be the Court of Appeal. Plainly, it is only in the superior courts that a divergence of view between judges in Great Britain and a Tribunal of Commissioners in Northern Ireland could ultimately be resolved and, in this instance, the relevant legislation had in fact already been amended so that any divergence in the law between Great Britain and Northern Ireland was going to be short-lived. It is arguable that those are the reasons why the single judge, being satisfied that the decision of the Tribunal of Commissioners was wrong, was justified in not following it. Had the Chamber President declined to convene a three-judge panel in a case where there was a relevant decision of a three-judge panel of the Upper Tribunal, the single judge would, it is suggested, have been obliged to follow it notwithstanding that new material had been advanced before him. Since a single judge cannot actually overrule a decision of a three-judge panel or even another decision of a single judge, the position otherwise would be that the First-tier Tribunal would be left to choose between the two decisions with there being scope for argument as to which was right despite one of them being a decision of a three-judge panel. Thus, this may actually be an example of a rare case where a decision of a Tribunal of Commissioners in Northern Ireland was not to be treated by a single judge in Great Britain in the same way as a decision of a three-judge panel of the Upper Tribunal.

p.1488, *annotation to the Tribunals, Courts and Enforcement Act 2007 s.7 (Chambers: jurisdiction and Presidents)*

4.045 With effect from October 1, 2015, art.2(1) and (3) of the First-tier Tribunal and Upper Tribunal (Chambers) Amendment Order 2015 (SI 2015/1563) amended art.6 of the 2010 Order by inserting after sub-para.(e)—

"(ea) appealable decisions within the meaning of section 56(3) of the Childcare Payments Act 2014;".

pp.1496–1505, *annotation to the Tribunals, Courts and Enforcement Act 2007 s.11(1) (Right to appeal to Upper Tribunal)*

4.046 There is no right of appeal against a ruling on an issue that did not actually arise in the case in question and was merely intended to give guidance in other cases, because there is no jurisdiction to give such a ruling and no party has a sufficient interest in it (*Re X (Court of Protection Practice)* [2015] EWCA Civ 599; [2016] 1 W.L.R. 227).

The meaning of "a point of law" is the same in Scotland as in England and Wales, but there are many different ways of expressing it. In *HMRC v Murray Group Holdings Ltd* [2015] CSIH 77, the Inner House of the Court of Session said—

"[42] Although the concept of appeal on a point of law might seem simple, it has given rise to considerable controversy; indeed in the well-known case of *Edwards v Bairstow*, [1956] AC 14, an appeal was taken to the House of Lords to adjudicate upon differences of approach that had developed between the Scottish and English courts. We are of opinion that an appeal on a point of law covers four different categories of case. The first of these categories is appeals on the general law: the content of its rules. In tax appeals these are largely statutory, but the interpretation of a particular statutory provision may be a matter of general law, and tax law also includes a number of general non-statutory rules, such as the redirection principle and the *Ramsay* principle, both of which are relevant to this case. The second category comprises appeals on the application of the law to the facts as found by the First-tier Tribunal. This is in our opinion a clear example of an appeal on a point of law: it is the application of the general rules to particular factual situations that defines the frontiers of a legal rule and thus its practical scope. Furthermore, it is the application of the general rules to particular facts that brings about the development of those rules to meet new situations. For these reasons we consider that an appeal on the application of the general law to a particular factual situation must be regarded as being on a point of law. This is illustrated by the facts of *Edwards v Bairstow*. There the House of Lords, reversing the decisions of the General Commissioners and lower courts, held that a transaction involving the acquisition of spinning plant, dividing it into lots and selling those lots at a profit was an adventure in the nature of trade. In holding otherwise, the Commissioners and the lower courts had misdirected themselves as to the meaning and proper application of the expression "adventure . . . in the nature of trade" found in the relevant taxing statute, the Income Tax Act 1918: see Lord Radcliffe at [1956] AC 36–37.

[43] The third category of appeal on a point of law is where the Tribunal has made a finding "for which there is no evidence or which is inconsistent with the evidence and contradictory of it": *IRC v Fraser*, 1942 SC 493, at 497–498, per LP Normand. This runs into a fourth category, comprising cases where the First-tier Tribunal has made a fundamental error in its approach to the case: for example, by asking the wrong question, or by taking account of manifestly irrelevant considerations, or by arriving at a decision that no reasonable tax tribunal could properly reach. In such cases we conceive that the Court of Session and the Upper Tribunal have power to interfere with the decision of the First-tier Tribunal as disclosing an error on a point of law: *Edwards v Bairstow*, per Lord Radcliffe at [1956] AC 36."

The Court also observed that decisions of the First-tier Tribunal   **4.047** relating to tax frequently involve elements of evaluation and judgment and that: "In general, a court, or the Upper Tribunal, should be slow to interfere with the decision of the First-tier Tribunal in cases of this nature." Nonetheless: "It is a matter of degree: the higher the factual component in the evaluative exercise, the slower the court should be to interfere, but correspondingly if the factual component is relatively low and the legal component is high the court may properly interfere."

Although the Court did not draw any distinction between the position of a court and the position of the Upper Tribunal, it is arguable that, since one of the reasons why appellate bodies do not interfere is the specialist nature of the First-tier Tribunal, there may be some cases where the Upper Tribunal can properly interfere but an appellate court would not, because the Upper Tribunal may be able to claim as much relevant expertise as the First-tier Tribunal. This point did not arise for consideration in that case because the Upper Tribunal dismissed the appeal from the First-tier Tribunal and the Court of Session decided that they were both wrong in law.

The Upper Tribunal's decision in *CM v SSWP (DLA)* [2013] UKUT 27 (AAC), mentioned in the main volume at p.1500, is not now to be reported in the Administrative Appeals Chamber Reports because there were further appeals to the Court of Appeal, which upheld the Upper Tribunal's decision, and then to the Supreme Court (*Mathieson Secretary of State for Work and Pensions* [2015] UKSC 47; [2015] 1 W.L.R. 3250; [2015] AACR 19), which held it to have been wrong in law. Neither court expressed any criticism of the Upper Tribunal having said that the question it had to decide was not whether the First-tier Tribunal had correctly directed itself but was simply whether there had been a breach of the European Convention on Human Rights. The Supreme Court did consider whether it should disagree with the view of the Upper Tribunal in the light of *AH (Sudan) v Secretary of State for the Home Department* [2007] UKHL 49; [2008] 1 A.C. 678 (see the annotation to s.13 in the main volume on p.1514) but, although the Upper Tribunal was a specialist tribunal, it had erred in law in its analysis. On a correct analysis, the Secretary of State had violated the claimant's human rights in suspending payment of disability living allowance and, since he had not been compelled by primary legislation to suspend payment, had acted unlawfully in doing so with the result that the First-tier Tribunal should have allowed the claimant's appeal and reinstated payment from the date from which it had been suspended. The Supreme Court therefore made a decision to that effect.

pp.1508–1511, *annotation to the Tribunals, Courts and Enforcement Act 2007 s.12 (Proceedings on appeal to Upper Tribunal)*

4.048   The question whether a case should be remitted to the First-tier Tribunal when the Upper Tribunal allows an appeal is often linked to the question whether either of the parties is entitled to an oral hearing for the purpose of resolving issued of fact, since the Administrative Appeals Chamber of the Upper Tribunal seldom holds oral hearings only for the purpose of hearing evidence. Thus, remittal will be appropriate if there are issues of credibility or reliability that a party has not had a satisfactory opportunity to address at an oral hearing (e.g., because although there was a hearing before the First-tier Tribunal the relevant findings cannot be relied upon in the light of the First-tier Tribunal's error of law) and it is not convenient for the Upper Tribunal to hold a hearing for the purpose of resolving the issues. See *JA (Ghana) v Secretary of State for the Home Department* [2015] EWCA Civ 1031 for a case where these points were considered in the context of an appeal from the Immigration and Asylum Chamber of the Upper Tribunal. It is consistent with the approach taken in *R(IB) 2/07* and *CDLA/4217/2001*, mentioned on p.1509 of the main volume.

It was also held in *JA (Ghana)* that, where the Upper Tribunal has made a finding of fact before remitting the case, the First-tier Tribunal is bound by that finding even if there is no specific direction to that effect. This is consistent with the approach taken in *Kuteh v Secretary of State for Education* [2014] EWCA Civ 1586, where it was held that the Upper Tribunal was bound by a finding made by the Administrative Court when quashing a decision before remitting a case. However, where a case is remitted by the Upper Tribunal to a panel of the First-tier Tribunal that is constituted differently from the panel whose decision has been set aside, the new panel is not entitled to adopt a finding made by the previous panel *only* because the Upper Tribunal has held that particular finding not to be vitiated by any error of law or has not commented on it, although it may adopt the finding for other reasons and must adopt it if directed to do so by the Upper Tribunal (*KK v SSWP (DLA)* [2015] UKUT 417 (AAC)).

As mentioned in the man volume, there is usually a practical advantage in a social security case being remitted to a differently constituted panel of the First-tier Tribunal rather than to the particular panel whose decision has been set aside. However, in the absence of any such practical advantage, it would still be wrong to remit a case to the same panel if that would give rise to "reasonably perceived unfairness to the affected parties" or "damage to the public confidence in the decision making process" (*HCA International Ltd v Competition and Markets Authority* [2015] EWCA Civ 492; [2015] 1 W.L.R. 4341).

A case to the same effect as *Nesbitt's Application* [2013] NIQB 111; [2014] AACR 31, mentioned in the main volume, is *Rochdale Metropolitan Borough Council v KW (No.2)* [2015] EWCA Civ 1054; [2016] 1 W.L.R. 198, where it was held that a judge of the Court of Protection had been bound by a consent order of the Court of Appeal and it was futile and inappropriate for him to seek to undermine it by complaining that it was ultra vires or wrong for any other reason.

pp.1513–1519, *annotation to the Tribunals, Courts and Enforcement Act 2007 s.13 (Right to appeal to Court of Appeal etc.)*

Sarfraz v Disclosure and Barring Service [2015] EWCA Civ 544; **4.049** [2015] AACR 35, mentioned on both p.1513 and p.1517 of the main volume, has been reported additionally at [2015] 1 W.L.R. 4441. *Mathieson v Secretary of State for Work and Pensions* [2015] UKSC 47; [2015] 1 W.L.R. 3250, mentioned on p.1515 of the main volume, has been reported additionally at [2015] AACR 19.

In *Secretary of State for Work and Pensions v Robertson* [2015] CSIH 82, the Court of Session held the appeal by the Secretary of State to be incompetent because the Secretary of State had been successful before the Upper Tribunal. Despite his success, the Secretary of State had wished to appeal because, in the course of its decision, the Upper Tribunal had held that a regulation was invalid and the Secretary of State considered that, unless the Court of Session held it to be wrong, he would be bound to follow that finding to the disadvantage of other claimants. The Court of Session held that, because it had not been necessary for the Upper Tribunal to consider whether the regulation was invalid and its finding on that point formed no part of its reason for dismissing the claimant's appeal, the point of law did not arise from the Upper Tribunal's decision. The implication is presumably that the Secretary of State had been wrong to consider that he would be obliged to follow the finding in other cases because it was only *obiter dicta*, although the Court of Session refrained from saying so on the ground that "how the appellant chooses to act is a matter for him".

For the meaning of "point of law" in Scotland, see *HMRC v Murray Group Holdings Ltd* [2015] CSIH 77 (considered in the supplementary annotation to s.11(1), above). This was another case, like *Revenue and Customs Commissioners v Pendragon plc* [2015] UKSC 37; [2015] 1 W.L.R. 2838 mentioned on p.1514 of the main volume, where it was difficult to decide whether the point in issue was a point of law or a point of fact).

4.050   Normally English and Welsh law is regarded as foreign law in Scotland (and *vice versa*) and so is treated as a matter of fact that has to be proved by evidence. However, where the First-tier Tribunal and Upper Tribunal exercise jurisdiction throughout Great Britain, they are taken to have judicial knowledge of both English and Welsh law and Scots law, wherever they are sitting, so that proof of the law of either part of Great Britain is unnecessary. It follows that, where the Court of Session hears an appeal from the Upper Tribunal in a tax case or social security case, it also is to be taken to have judicial knowledge of English and Welsh law (*HMRC v Murray Group Holdings Ltd* [2015] CSIH 77 at [50]).

The Court of Session takes the same approach to admitting new grounds of appeal as the Court of Appeal (*HMRC v Murray Group Holdings Ltd* [2015] CSIH 77 at [39], where reference was made to *Miskovic v Secretary of State for Work and Pensions* [2011] EWCA Civ 16; [2012] AACR 11 which is mentioned on p.1515 of the main volume).

That the Appeals from the Upper Tribunal to the Court of Appeal Order 2008 (SI 2008/2834), mentioned in the main volume, applies only to cases where the case before the Upper Tribunal was an appeal from the First-tier Tribunal has been confirmed in *Clarise Properties Ltd v Rees* [2015] EWCA Civ 1118, where the appeal to the Upper Tribunal had been from the Leasehold Valuation Tribunal for Wales.

Although there is no right of appeal against a refusal of the Upper Tribunal to give permission to appeal to itself, it has been held in the context of analogous legislation relating to appeals from a county court (under which there was no right of appeal to the Court of Appeal from a decision of a circuit judge refusing permission to appeal to himself from a decision of a district judge) that there is a right of appeal against a decision to strike out an application for permission to appeal to a circuit judge and that, in the circumstances of the case, an order drawn as a dismissal of an application for permission to appeal was in fact a striking out of the application so that an appeal lay to the Court of Appeal (*Patel v Mussa* [2015] EWCA Civ 434; [2015] 1 W.L.R. 4788).

pp.1520-1521, *annotation to the Tribunals, Courts and Enforcement Act 2007, s.14 (Proceedings on appeal to Court of Appeal etc.)*

In *Rochdale Metropolitan Borough Council v KW (No.2)* [2015] EWCA Civ 1054; [2016] 1 W.L.R. 198, it was held that a judge of the Court of Protection had been bound by a consent order of the Court of Appeal and it was futile and inappropriate for him to seek to undermine it by complaining that it was ultra vires or wrong for any other reason. The Court also explained that, although the question whether the Court would allow a decision by consent on the papers without determining the merits would depend on the circumstances, it was likely to do so if satisfied that the parties' consent to allow the appeal was based on apparently competent legal advice and if the parties had advanced plausible reasons to show that the decision of the lower court was wrong. However, it would not do so if, for instance, the decision of the lower court had been reported and was causing difficulties. 4.050.1

p.1528, *insertion of the Tribunals, Courts and Enforcement Act 2007 s.20A (Procedural steps where application for judicial review transferred to the Upper Tribunal from the Court of Session)*

With effect from September 22, 2015, art.7 of the Courts Reform (Scotland) Act 2014 (Consequential Provisions and Modifications) Order 2015 (SI 2015/700) inserted after s.20 of the 2007 Act— 4.051

"Procedural steps where application transferred

20A.—(1) This section applies where the Court of Session transfers an application under section 20(1).
(2) It is for the Upper Tribunal to determine—
(a) whether the application has been made timeously, and
(b) whether to grant permission for the application to proceed under section 27B of the Court of Session Act 1988 ("the 1988 Act") (requirement for permission).
(3) Accordingly—
(a) the Upper Tribunal has the same powers in relation to the application as the Court of Session would have had in relation to it under sections 27A to 27C of the 1988 Act,
(b) sections 27C and 27D of that Act apply in relation to a decision of the Upper Tribunal under section 27B(1) of that Act as they apply in relation to such a decision of the Court of Session.
(4) The references in section 27C(3) and (4) of the 1988 Act (oral hearings where permission refused) to a different Lord Ordinary from the one who granted or refused permission are to be read as references

to different members of the Tribunal from those of whom it was composed when it refused or granted permission."

This follows from the coming into force of s.89 of the Courts Reform (Scotland) Act 2014 (an Act of the Scottish Parliament), which inserted ss.27A to 27D into the Court of Session Act 1988 and so introduces a requirement that applicants for judicial review in Scotland obtain permission, as in England and Wales. The procedure under ss.27A to 27D is similar to the procedure in England and Wales, but is not identical not although there has not been any amendment to the Tribunal Procedure (Upper Tribunal) Rules 2008.

pp.1532–1533, *annotation to the Tribunals, Courts and Enforcement Act 2007 s.25 (Supplementary powers of Upper Tribunal)*

4.052 Where a power is conferred specifically on the "High Court" by statute, s.25 cannot be read as having the effect that the Upper Tribunal may also exercise the power. The Upper Tribunal therefore has no power to award *pro bono* costs by virtue of s.194 of the Legal Services Act 2007 (*Raftopoulou v HMRC* [2015] UKUT 630 (TCC)).

p.1535, *annotation to the Tribunals, Courts and Enforcement Act 2007 s.29(1)–(3) (Costs or expenses)*

4.053 This section does not empower the First-tier Tribunal or Upper Tribunal to order a sum of money to be paid to a prescribed charity (usually an organisation providing *pro bono* representation) where a party being represented *pro bono* has not actually incurred costs or expenses due to the conduct of another party but an order would have been made if the first party had been paying for representation (*Raftopoulou v HMRC* [2015] UKUT 630 (TCC)). Some courts in England and Wales have such a power under s.194 of the Legal Services Act 2007, but that provision does not apply to tribunals.

pp.1559–1561, *amendment to the Tribunal Procedure (First-tier Tribunal) (Social Entitlement Chamber) Rules 2008 (SI 2008/2685) r.1(3) (Interpretation)*

4.054 With effect from August 21, 2015, rr.11 and 12 of the Tribunal Procedure (Amendment) Rules 2015 (SI 2015/1510) amended the definition of "respondent" by omitting "or" after sub-para.(c) and inserting—

"(cc) an affected party within the meaning of section 61(5) of the Childcare Payments Act 2014, other than an appellant; or".

pp.1565–1566, *amendment to the Procedure (First-tier Tribunal) (Social Entitlement Chamber) Rules 2008 (SI 2008/2685) r.5(3) (case management powers)*

4.055 With effect from August 21, 2015, rr.11 and 13 of the Tribunal Procedure (Amendment) Rules 2015 (SI 2015/1510) revoked r.5(3)(aa) of the 2008 Rules, because reg.28(1) of the Child Benefit and Guardian's Allowance Regulations 2003 had ceased to have any transitional effect in relation to Great Britain.

pp.1568–1572, *annotation to the Tribunal Procedure (First-tier Tribunal) (Social Entitlement Chamber) Rules 2008 (SI 2008/2685) r.5(3)(f), (g) and (h) (case management powers—hearings)*

It is pointed out in *LO v SSWP (ESA)* [2016] UKUT 10 (AAC) that **4.055** the duty to make reasonable adjustments in order to avoid discrimination under the Equality Act 2010 is disapplied in relation to judicial functions by para.3 of Sch.3 to that Act and so to that extent the reasoning in *DC v SSWP (ESA)* [2014] UKUT 218 (AAC), mentioned in the main volume, is unsatisfactory. However, this may not make much practical difference because the same consideration apply to the general duty to act fairly in exercising judicial functions. In *LO*, was also given to whether, where a claimant states that he or she does not wish to attend a hearing because of disability, a tribunal ought generally to consider whether a telephone hearing would be appropriate. The judge rejected a submission that it was unnecessary to do so merely because the claimant had not asked for such a hearing, because it was not the practice of the First-tier Tribunal's administration to inform parties of the possibility of there being a telephone hearing and so claimants could not be expected to ask for one. However, he held that there had been no error of law in the particular case before him. The First-tier Tribunal had given detailed consideration to the question whether there needed to be an adjournment so that the claimant could give evidence and had taken a proportionate approach. Although an offer of a telephone hearing was one possibility that might have been considered, it had not been necessary to do so in that case in order the deal with the issue of adjournment fairly. The claimant might, after all, have declined such an offer. However, the implication of the decision is that there may be at least some cases where a failure explicitly to consider whether to offer a telephone hearing will render a decision wrong in law.

pp.1572–1573, *annotation to the Tribunal Procedure (First-tier Tribunal) (Social Entitlement Chamber) Rules 2008 (SI 2008/2685) r.5(3)(l) (Case management powers—suspension of decision)*

In the main volume it is stated that, although the First-tier Tribunal **4.056** has no power to suspend the effect of a decision being challenged on appeal to it, judicial review proceedings may be brought in the Administrative Court or the Court of Session in non-social security cases to achieve a suspension pending an appeal. However, in *CC & C Ltd v Revenue and Customs Commissioners* [2014] EWCA Civ 1653; [2015] 1 W.L.R. 4043, it was held that, while a court before whom parallel judicial review proceedings challenging the decision against which an appeal had been brought had the formal power to grant interim relief having the effect of suspending the decision until the First-tier Tribunal heard the appeal, it should exercise the power only if it was arguable that the decision was unlawful on a fundamental basis such as being an abuse of power or improper or taken in bad faith, rather than merely being unreasonable. Whether that distinction is important, or whether that case can be distinguished, in the context of social security and other welfare law appeals remains to be determined.

pp.1577–1581, *annotation to the Tribunal Procedure (First-tier Tribunal) (Social Entitlement Chamber) Rules 2008 (SI 2008/2685) r.8 (Striking out a party's case)*

4.057 In relation to ordinary civil proceedings, the Court of Appeal has reiterated the point that a judge considering on the papers whether to strike out a case should avoid conducting a mini-trial and should not determine issues of credibility "where oral evidence at least *might* have put a different complexion on the allegations made" (emphasis of the Court). Moreover, it was said that a case should be struck out on the ground that there has been a breach of a rule, practice direction or order only if that would be a proportionate response to the breach (*Alpha Rocks Solicitors v Alade* [2015] EWCA Civ 685; [2015] 1 W.L.R. 4534). Permission to appeal to the Supreme Court was refused. The need to enforce rules was, however, given greater weight in *Thevarajah v Riordan* [2015] UKSC 78; [2016] 1 W.L.R. 76, a decision in respect of relief from sanction (in the form of barring the defendant from defending the claim), where it was held that belated compliance with an "unless" order equivalent to the type of direction mentioned in r.8(1) could not amount to a change of circumstances justifying relief unless accompanied by other facts. It is, perhaps, arguable that the express and unqualified power of reinstatement conferred by r.8(5) and the different content of cases before the First-tier Tribunal suggest that a less strict approach is appropriate under these Rules.

Interestingly the Court of Appeal in that case said that it was "troubled by the deputy judge's observation that even if the respondents remained debarred from defending the claim they would be 'entitled at trial to require the claimant to prove his claim, to cross-examine and make submissions'" (*Thevarajah v Riordan* [2014] EWCA Civ 14 at [38]). However, it was not necessary for it to decide that point and the Supreme Court did not do so either.

The desirability of conveying judicial decisions to the parties in a form that shows not only that they have been made by a judge but also by which judge and when they were made has been emphasised in *JP v SSWP (ESA)* [2016] UKUT 48 (AAC).

p.1589, *annotation to the Tribunal Procedure (First-tier Tribunal) (Social Entitlement Chamber) Rules 2008 (SI 2008/2685) r.14(1) (Use of documents and information)*

4.058 *Re X (Reporting restriction order: Variation)* [2015] UKUT 380 (AAC), mentioned in the main volume, is to be reported at [2016] AACR 6. In that case, a local authority that had not been a party to proceedings before the Upper Tribunal in which an order had been made under r.14(1) of the Tribunal Procedure (Upper Tribunal) Rules 2008, but was aware of them, sought permission to disclose information relating to the proceedings to the police. Applying guidance given by the Court of Appeal in relation to care proceedings in *Re C (A Minor) (Care Proceedings: Disclosure)* [1997] Fam 76, the order prohibiting publication of any matter likely to lead members of the public to identify certain adults and children was varied so as to permit disclosure of the decision of the Upper Tribunal and the identities of individuals mentioned in it to the police and other relevant bodies for the limited purposes of investigating criminal offences, bringing prosecutions and protecting any child or vulnerable adult.

pp.1593-1594, *annotation to the Tribunal Procedure (First-tier Tribunal) (Social Entitlement Chamber) Rules 2008 (SI 2008/2685) r.16 (summoning or citation of witnesses and orders to answer questions or produce documents)*

The desirability of conveying judicial decisions to the parties in a form   **4.058.1**
that shows not only that they have been made by a judge but also by which judge and when they were made has been emphasised in *JP v SSWP (ESA)* [2016] UKUT 48 (AAC).

p.1594, *substitution of the Tribunal Procedure (First-tier Tribunal) (Social Entitlement Chamber) Rules 2008 (SI 2008/2685) r.17(4) and (5) (Withdrawal)*

With effect from August 21, 2015, the Tribunal Procedure (Amend-   **4.059**
ment) Rules 2015 (SI 2015/1510) rr.11 and 14 amended r.17 of the 2008 Rules by substituting for paras (4) and (5)—

"(4) An application for a withdrawn case to be reinstated may be made by—
  (a) the party who withdrew the case;
  (b) where an appeal in a social security and child support case has been withdrawn, a respondent.
(5) An application under paragraph (4) must be made in writing and be received by the Tribunal within 1 month after the earlier of—
  (a) the date on which the applicant was sent notice under paragraph (6) that the withdrawal had taken effect; or
  (b) if the applicant was present at the hearing when the case was withdrawn orally under paragraph (1)(b), the date of that hearing.".

pp.1594–1595, *annotation to the Tribunal Procedure (First-tier Tribunal) (Social Entitlement Chamber) Rules 2008 (SI 2008/2685) r.17 (withdrawal)*

The amendment noted above enables a respondent (who might be   **4.060**
the decision maker but might be a third party where, for instance,

there has been a joint claim or the case concerns child support maintenance) to object to the withdrawal of a social security or child support appeal. A respondent might wish to do so where he or she might be unfairly prejudiced by having to make a new application for supersession or lodge a new appeal or make a new decision, as the case might be, due to the limits on the backdating of supersession decisions and the time limits for appeals. Making such an application for supersession, lodging an appeal or making a decision would usually have been unnecessary while the other proceedings were effective.

In *WM v SSWP (DLA)* [2015] UKUT 642 (AAC), the Upper Tribunal made it plain that, since the amendment to r.17(1) in 2013, a withdrawal made otherwise than at a hearing is automatically effective unless the First-tier Tribunal has given a direction under para.(3)(b) and that, where a hearing is adjourned, a notice of withdrawal given during the period of the adjournment is not given "at a hearing" for the purposes of para.(3)(c). Thus the First-tier Tribunal had no power to decline to accept the withdrawal and so had no jurisdiction to make a decision on the appeal that was less favourable to the claimant than the Secretary of State's decision. The judge also held that "rising to eat lunch . . . does not constitute a formal adjournment of the proceedings" and so does not interrupt the hearing for the purposes of this rule; it is only adjournment from one day to another that interrupts a hearing. It is in this sort of case that the amendment made from August 21, 2015 (see above) is relevant. The Secretary of State may now apply for a withdrawn appeal to be reinstated if he considers (e.g., in the light of evidence that emerged in the appeal proceedings before the appeal was withdrawn or in the light of an observation by the First-tier Tribunal) that the decision that was the subject of the appeal was too generous to the claimant but he is unable either to revise it or to supersede it with effect from a sufficiently early date. However, it is suggested that the conduct of both parties may be relevant and that an appeal should not necessarily be reinstated if the Secretary of State was clearly at fault in making the original decision and the claimant was blameless: in other words, it is suggested that the First-tier Tribunal should consider whether reinstatement would be fair in all the circumstances of the case. It is also suggested that reinstatement will seldom be desirable where the Secretary of State could achieve the same result by revising the original decision against which the claimant would have a fresh right of appeal.

pp.1598–1599, *amendments to the Tribunal Procedure (First-tier Tribunal) (Social Entitlement Chamber) Rules 2008 (SI 2008/2685) r.22 (Cases in which the notice of appeal is to be sent to the Tribunal)*

4.061   With effect from August 21, 2015, rr.11 and 15 of the Tribunal Procedure (Amendment) Rules 2015 (SI 2015/1510) amended r.22 of the 2008 Rules.

In para.(2)(d)(ii), for "(time specified for providing notice of appeal)", there is substituted "(time limits for providing notices of appeal in social security and child support cases where mandatory reconsideration does not apply)". This merely reflects the heading of Sch.1 as now substituted (see below).

Also, after paragraph (7) there is inserted—

"(7A) Her Majesty's Revenue and Customs must, upon receipt of the notice of appeal from the Tribunal under the Childcare Payments Act 2014, inform the Tribunal whether there are any affected parties within the meaning of section 61(5) of that Act other than the appellant and, if so, provide their names and addresses."

In most social security and child support cases, an appellant can be expected to know of, and name, any other respondent, even if unaware of his or her address. This is required by para.(3)(d) but, even if the other respondent is not named, the First-tier Tribunal is likely to be aware that there is another respondent. The First-tier Tribunal can therefore be expected to request any unknown details of the respondent from the decision-maker. However, in appeals under the Childcare Payments Act 2014, an appellant and the First-tier Tribunal may be wholly unaware that there are other affected parties. The onus is therefore placed on HMRC to inform the First-tier Tribunal of any such party, without the First-tier Tribunal first raising the issue.

Finally, for paragraph (9), there is substituted—

"(9) For the purposes of this rule, mandatory reconsideration applies where—
(a) the notice of the decision being challenged includes a statement to the effect that there is a right of appeal in relation to the decision only if the decision-maker has considered an application for the revision, reversal, review or reconsideration (as the case may be) of the decision being challenged; or
(b) the appeal is brought against a decision made by Her Majesty's Revenue and Customs.".

This amendment is made because legislation conferring rights of appeal against HMRC decisions has the effect that there is always a requirement to apply for reconsideration before appealing, even if HMRC has neglected to provide information to that effect in the notice of decision.

p.1602, *amendments to the Tribunal Procedure (First-tier Tribunal) (Social Entitlement Chamber) Rules 2008 (SI 2008/2685) r.23 (Cases in which the notice of appeal is to be sent to the decision maker)*

With effect from August 21, 2015, rr.11 and 16 of the Tribunal Procedure (Amendment) Rules 2015 (SI 2015/1510) amended r.23 of the 2008 Rules.   4.062

The first amendment makes explicit the fact that the rule now applies only to appeals relating to housing benefit, council tax benefit (in relation to entitlement before it was abolished) and child trust funds (where the possibility of an appeal is more theoretical than real). Thus, in para.(1), for the words from "social security" to the end of the paragraph, there is substituted "appeals under paragraph 6 of Schedule 7 to the Child Support, Pensions and Social Security Act 2000 (housing benefit and council tax benefit: revisions and appeals) or under section 22 of the Child Trust Funds Act 2004".

Secondly, the time limits for appeals are moved from Sch.1 (which now applies only to r.22) into this rule. Thus, in para.(2), for the words "within the time specified in Schedule 1 to these Rules (time limits for providing notices of appeal to the decision maker)", there is substituted—

"no later than the latest of—
    (a) in a housing benefit or council tax benefit case—
        (i) one month after the date on which notice of the decision being challenged was sent to the appellant;
        (ii) if a written statement of reasons for the decision was requested within that month, 14 days after the later of—
            (aa) the end of that month; or
            (ab) the date on which the written statement of reasons was provided; or
        (iii) if the appellant made an application for revision of the decision under regulation 4(1)(a) of the Housing Benefit and Council Tax Benefit (Decisions and Appeals) Regulations 2001 and that application was unsuccessful, one month after the date on which notice that the decision would not be revised was sent to the appellant;
    (b) in an appeal under section 22 of the Child Trust Funds Act 2004, the period of 30 days specified in section 23(1) of that Act.".

4.063   Consequentially, in para.(3), for "paragraph (2)", there is substituted "paragraph (2)(a)" and, in each of paras (4), (5) and (7)(a) and (b), for "Schedule 1" there is substituted "paragraph (2)". Although appeals in relation to housing benefit are outside the scope of this work, it may be noted, firstly that in para.(2)(a)(iii) there is now a reference to reg.4(1)(a) of the 2001 Regulations rather than simply to reg.4 as had been the case in Sch.1 and, secondly, that there appears to be a drafting error in that the words "the latest of" in the opening words of para.(2) should presumably be in the opening words of sub-para.(a) rather than where they are. For the significance of the first of those points, see the annotation to the substituted version of Sch.1 (below).

Finally, in para.(8), the words "or (aa)" are omitted because r.5(3)(aa) has been revoked (see above).

Note that, by virtue of r.18 of the 2015 Rules, the amendments to r.23 of, and the substitution of Sch.1 to, the 2008 Rules "have no effect in relation to any appeal against a decision made before 6th April 2014 where the decision maker was Her Majesty's Revenue and Customs". This saving makes explicit what would probably be the position anyway: any such appeal must be referred to the First-tier Tribunal which will refuse to admit it on the ground that it is irremediably out of time (unless to do so would be a breach of the European Convention on Human Rights—see the annotation to r.22(8) of the 2008 Rules in the main volume).

pp.1605–1607, *annotation to the Tribunal Procedure (First-tier Tribunal) (Social Entitlement Chamber) Rules 2008 (SI 2008/2685) r.24(1)-(5) (Responses)*

In *FN v SSWP (ESA)* [2015] UKUT 670 (AAC), a three-judge panel **4.064** has broadly agreed with *JC v DSD (IB)* [2011] NICom 177; [2014] AACR 30 and also both *ST v SSWP (ESA)* [2012] UKUT 469 (AAC) and *AM v SSWP (ESA)* [2013] UKUT 458 (AAC) (all mentioned in the main volume) but has stressed that the previous adjudication history and associated evidence is not always relevant to an employment and support allowance appeal and that, even if the Secretary of State has not produced all the information and evidence that he should have produced with his response to an appeal, it does not necessarily follow that the First-tier Tribunal's decision will be wrong in law and liable to be set aside.

"79. . . . We can envisage a situation where a First-tier Tribunal considers that it has sufficient relevant evidence before it to determine the issues arising in the appeal without the requirement to call for evidence which is missing because the Secretary of State has failed in his duty to provide it.

80. . . . Our view is that the first choice for the tribunal should not be to adjourn but to get on with the task of determining the issues arising in the appeal when satisfied that it has the necessary relevant evidence before it. It might be the case that having weighed and assessed the appellant's oral evidence, the tribunal might be satisfied that the evidence is credible, should be accepted and the appeal be allowed. . . . "

It is suggested that the question for the First-tier Tribunal is not just whether it has sufficient evidence to enable it to determine the issues before it but whether it has sufficient evidence to do so *fairly* in a case where the evidence before it leads it towards a decision adverse to the claimant. This may involve an assessment of the probable helpfulness to the claimant of evidence that the Secretary of State could produce but has not produced. Even if the First-tier Tribunal reasonably decides to proceed in the absence of previous medical reports that it considers the Secretary of State should have produced, it is arguable that, if it decides the case against the claimant, its decision may be set aside for inadvertent procedural error (either under r.37 or on review or appeal) if it transpires that the reports that should have been produced would substantially have supported the claimant's case.

Because good administration requires that citizens be treated in accor- **4.065** dance with a policy adopted by a Government department unless there are good reasons for not doing so, a respondent to an appeal to the First-tier Tribunal fails in his or her duty to draw relevant matters to the attention of the tribunal if no mention is made of a policy favourable to the appellant in the response to the appeal (*Mandalia v Secretary of State for the Home Department* [2015] UKSC 59; [2015] 1 W.L.R. 4546). This is relevant where the decision under appeal involved exercising an element of discretion or at least judgment and there is published guidance as to how the discretion or judgment should be exercised. It is presumably not necessary to refer to the policy document itself if the submission is in accordance with it, but a decision of the First-tier Tribunal may well be set aside if the First-tier Tribunal makes a decision that is adverse to a claimant but is inconsistent with a published policy unless a good reason for departing from the policy has been given (see, for instance, *SB v Oxford CC (HB)* [2014] UKUT 166 (AAC)). That is most likely to happen if a policy is not drawn to the attention of the First-tier Tribunal.

pp.1615–1617, *annotation to the Tribunal Procedure (First-tier Tribunal) (Social Entitlement Chamber) Rules 2008 (SI 2008/2685) r.27(1)-(2) (Hearing—record of proceedings)*

4.066   In *DT v SSWP (II)* [2015] UKUT 509 (AAC), the Upper Tribunal set aside a decision of the First-tier Tribunal for failing to keep a record of proceedings in a case where the grounds of appeal contained allegations as to the conduct of the hearing and a record of the proceedings, which would have been material, had apparently been destroyed six months after the First-tier Tribunal had given its decision but just before it produced its very late statement of reasons. It was held that the practice statement set out in the annotation in the main volume imposed a duty to keep the record of proceedings for more than six months after the date of decision where a statement of reasons had been requested but not provided within that period and that the breach of that duty amounted to a material error of law because it made it impossible fairly to adjudicate on the claimant's grounds of appeal. There may in fact have been a simple administrative error in this case because, as noted in the main volume, it is the practice of Her Majesty's Courts and Tribunals Service to keep the file, including any record of proceedings, for six months from the last action on the file, and correspondence with the judge who should have been providing the statement of reasons would normally have counted as relevant action. It appears that the proceedings had been digitally recorded but that the recording was not in the file that had been sent to the Upper Tribunal and it therefore seems probable that administrative staff either did not recognise that the request by the Upper Tribunal for the record of proceedings (which often consists of the judge's hand-written notes) was a request for that recording or else did not know where to find it.

pp.1620–1621, *annotation to the Tribunal Procedure (First-tier Tribunal) (Social Entitlement Chamber) Rules 2008 (SI 2008/2685) r.30(3) (Decision with or without a hearing)*

4.067   Even in the courts, it is recognised that the confidential nature of documents that must be considered at a hearing may justify holding the hearing in private (see, for instance, *Eurasian Natural Resources Corporation Ltd v Dechert LLP* [2014] EWHC 3389 (Ch); [2015] 1 W.L.R. 4621).

pp.1623–1624, *annotation to the Tribunal Procedure (First-tier Tribunal) (Social Entitlement Chamber) Rules 2008 (SI 2008/2685) r.31 (Hearings in a party's absence)*

In *JH(S) v SSWP (ESA)* [2015] UKUT 567 (AAC), the Upper Tribunal rejected a submission by the Secretary of State to the effect that the First-tier Tribunal had erred in law in overlooking the Senior President of Tribunals' *Practice Direction (First-tier and Upper Tribunals: Children, Vulnerable Adults and Sensitive Witnesses)*. The Upper Tribunal took the view that the Tribunal Procedure Rules, common law and the European Convention on Human Rights required the First-tier Tribunal to have regard to substantially the same considerations as the Practice Direction and the First-tier Tribunal had not erred in its decision to proceed in the claimant's absence despite not referring to the Practice Direction.   **4.068**

p.1625, *annotation to the Tribunal Procedure (First-tier Tribunal) (Social Entitlement Chamber) Rules 2008 (SI 2008/2685) r.33(1) (Notice of decisions)*

In *Patel v Secretary of State for the Home Department* [2015] EWCA Civ 1175, the Court of Appeal held that that a tribunal had no power to change a decision after it had been given orally. It said that the rule in the courts that a decision could be amended until an order was drawn up did not apply in tribunal where there is simply a decision and no distinction between a judgment and an order, it being relevant that there was an express power to give a decision orally. The Court appears not to have been referred to the power of the Upper Tribunal to set aside decisions (equivalent to r.37 of these Rules), which might have been relevant in that case, but that does not undermine the main thrust of its decision.   **4.068.1**

pp.1649–1650, *substitution of the Tribunal Procedure (First-tier Tribunal) (Social Entitlement Chamber) Rules 2008 (SI 2008/2685) Sch.1 (Time limits for providing notices of appeal).*

With effect from August 21, 2015, the Tribunal Procedure (Amendment) Rules 2015 (SI 2015/1510) rr.11 and 17 and Sch. substituted for the existing Sch.1 to the 2008 Rules—   **4.069**

Rule 22

SCHEDULE 1

Time Limits for providing notices of appeal in social security and child support cases where mandatory reconsideration does not apply

Type of proceedings	Time for providing notice of appeal
1 Appeal against a certification of NHS charges under section 157(1) of the Health and Social Care (Community Health and Standards) Act 2003	(a) 3 months after the latest of— (i) the date on the certificate; (ii) the date on which the compensation payment was made;

Type of proceedings	Time for providing notice of appeal
	(iii) if the certificate has been reviewed, the date the certificate was confirmed or a fresh certificate was issued; or (iv) the date of any agreement to treat an earlier compensation payment as having been made in final discharge of a claim made by or in respect of an injured person and arising out of the injury or death; or (b) if the person to whom the certificate has been issued makes an application under section 157(4) of the Health and Social Care (Community Health and Standards) Act 2003, one month after— (i) the date of the decision on that application; or (ii) if the person appeals against that decision under section 157(6) of that Act, the date on which the appeal is decided or withdrawn.
2 Appeal against a waiver decision under section 157(6) of the Health and Social Care (Community Health and Standards) Act 2003	One month after the date of the decision.
3 Appeal against a certificate of NHS charges under section 7 of the Road Traffic (NHS Charges) Act 1999	3 months after the latest of— (a) the date on which the liability under section 1(2) of the Road Traffic (NHS Charges) Act 1999 was discharged; (b) if the certificate has been reviewed, the date the certificate was confirmed or a fresh certificate was issued; or (c) the date of any agreement to treat an earlier compensation payment as having been made in final discharge of a claim made by or in respect of a traffic casualty and arising out of the injury or death.
4 Appeal against a certificate of recoverable benefits under section 11 of the Social Security (Recovery of Benefits) Act 1997	One month after the latest of— (a) the date on which any payment to the Secretary of State required under section 6 of the Social Security (Recovery of Benefits) Act 1997 was made; (b) if the certificate has been reviewed, the date the certificate was confirmed or a fresh certificate was issued; (c) the date of any agreement to treat an earlier compensation payment as having been made in final discharge of a claim made by or in respect of an injured person and arising out of the accident, injury or disease.

Type of proceedings	Time for providing notice of appeal

5 Cases other than those listed above	The latest of—
	(a) one month after the date on which notice of the decision being challenged was sent to the appellant;
	(b) if a written statement of reasons for the decision was requested within that month, 14 days after the later of—
	    (i) the end of that month; or
	    (ii) the date on which the written statement of reasons was provided;
	(c) if the appellant made an application for the revision of the decision under—
	    (i) regulation 17(1)(a) of the Child Support (Maintenance Assessment Procedure) Regulations 1992;
	    (ii) regulation 3(1) or (3) or 3A(1)(a) of the Social Security and Child Support (Decisions and Appeals) Regulations 1999;
	    (iii) regulation 14(1)(a) of the Child Support Maintenance Calculation Regulations 2012; or
	    (iv) regulation 5 of the Universal Credit, Personal Independence Payment, Jobseeker's Allowance and Employment and Support Allowance (Decisions and Appeals) Regulations 2013,
	and the application was unsuccessful, one month after the date on which notice that the decision would not be revised was sent to the appellant.

4.070 Originally, Sch.1 applied just for the purposes of r.23 but, from April 2013 (i.e., during the transition to direct lodgement), it applied both to r.22 and r.23. Now, the time limits for r.23 have been incorporated into that rule and the Schedule applies only in the few cases where a notice of appeal in a social security or child support appeals must be sent to the First-tier Tribunal under r.22 but there is no requirement to apply for reconsideration before lodging the appeal.

The first three paragraphs deal with cases concerned with the recovery of NHS charges, which are beyond the scope of this work but where the legislation makes no provision for mandatory reconsideration. Paragraphs 4 and 5 deal with other social security and child support cases where there is no mandatory reconsideration. This will usually be because the Secretary of State has, either by accident or design, not provided the requisite notice with the decision being challenged (see, in relation to social security cases, regs 3ZA(1) and 9ZB(1) of the Social Security and Child Support (Decisions and Appeals) Regulations 1999, set out in the main volume).

Note that, in addition to the re-ordering of the paragraphs and the deletion of those that are now unnecessary, there have been substantive amendments to what is now head (c) in the second column of para.5. First, a reference to the 2013 Regulations has been added, while the reference to housing benefit and council tax benefit legislation has been moved to r.23(2)(a)(iii). Secondly, each of the references to child support legislation is now to sub-para.(a) of para.(1) of the relevant provision, rather than just to para.(1). This gives statutory effect to *AS v SSWP (CSM)* [2012] UKUT 448 (AAC); [2013] AACR 18 (mentioned in the annotation in the main volume) and explicitly brings child support cases into line with social security cases so that the time for appealing is automatically extended where there has been an unsuccessful revision only if the application for revision was made within one month (or any longer period allowed by the Secretary of State) of the decision being challenged. A similar amendment has been made in what is now r.23(2)(a)(iii) (see above).

p.1655, *contents of the Tribunal Procedure (Upper Tribunal) Rules 2008 (SI 2008/2698)*

4.071 The following entry has been omitted in error—

"48. Power to treat an application as a different type of application From August 21, 2015, there is also a Sch.A1 (see below)."

pp.1656–1660, *amendments to the Tribunal Procedure (Upper Tribunal) Rules 2008 (SI 2008/2698) r.1(3) (Interpretation)*

4.072 With effect from August 21, 2015, rr.2 and 3 of the Tribunal Procedure (Amendment) Rules 2015 (SI 2015/1510) inserted definitions of "QCS Board", "quality contracts scheme" and "quality contracts scheme case" and amended the definition of "special educational needs case". None of these definitions is relevant to social security cases and so they are not set out here.

In *R. (Detention Action) v First-tier Tribunal (Immigration and Asylum Chamber)* [2015] EWCA Civ 840; [2015] 1 W.L.R. 5341, the Court of Appeal dismissed an appeal against a decision of the High Court in which the special rules for fast-track cases were quashed on the ground that they were unfair and unjust and therefore unlawful.

pp.1673–1674, *annotation to the Tribunal Procedure (Upper Tribunal) Rules 2008 (SI 2008/2698) r.10 (Orders for costs)*

4.073 In *R(MM and DM) v SSWP (Costs)* [2015] UKUT 566 (AAC), a three-judge panel has held that, in judicial review cases transferred to the Upper Tribunal from the High Court, costs are to be awarded in accordance with the principles that would be applied in the High Court.

The Upper Tribunal has no power akin to that conferred on some courts in England and Wales by s.194 of the Legal Services Act 2007 to order a sum of money to be paid to a prescribed charity (usually an organisation providing *pro bono* representation) where a party being represented *pro bono* has not actually incurred costs or expenses due to the conduct of another party but an order would have been made if the first party had been paying for representation (*Raftopoulou v HMRC* [2015] UKUT 630 (TCC)).

p.1680, *annotation to the Tribunal Procedure (Upper Tribunal) Rules 2008 (SI 2008/2698) r.14(1) (Use of documents and information)*

Re X (Reporting restriction order: Variation) [2015] UKUT 380 (AAC), mentioned in the main volume, is to be reported at [2016] AACR 6. In that case, a local authority that had been involved in, but had not been a party to, proceedings in which an order had been made under r.14(1), prohibiting publication of any matter likely to lead members of the public to identify certain adults and children, sought permission to disclose information relating to the proceedings to the police. Applying guidance given by the Court of Appeal in relation to care proceedings in *Re C (A Minor) (Care Proceedings: Disclosure)* [1997] Fam 76, the order was varied so as to permit disclosure of the decision of the Upper Tribunal and the identities of individuals mentioned in it to the police and other relevant bodies for the limited purposes of investigating criminal offences, bringing prosecutions and protecting any child or vulnerable adult.

4.074

p.1691, *annotation to the Tribunal Procedure (Upper Tribunal) Rules 2008 (SI 2008/2698) r.22(2) (Decision in relation to permission to appeal)*

In *Patel v Secretary of State for the Home Department* [2015] EWCA Civ 1175, the Court of Appeal held that that a tribunal had no power to change a decision after it had been given orally. It said that the rule in the courts that a decision could be amended until an order was drawn up did not apply in tribunal where there is simply a decision and no distinction between a judgment and an order, it being relevant that there was an express power in r.40(1) to give a decision orally. Therefore, when a judge had said that he was granting permission to appeal, he could not later during the hearing consider whether he should refuse to admit the application for permission because it was late. The Court appears not to have been referred to the power of the Upper Tribunal to set aside decisions under r.43, which might have been relevant in that case, but that does not undermine the main thrust of its decision.

4.074.1

pp.1691–1692, *amendments to the Tribunal Procedure (Upper Tribunal) Rules 2008 (SI 2008/2698) r.23 (Notice of appeal)*

With effect from August 21, 2015, rr.2 and 4 of the Tribunal Procedure (Amendment) Rules 2015 (SI 2015/1510) substituted for para. 2(b)—

4.075

> "(b) if permission to appeal is not required, the date on which notice of decision to which the appeal relates—
>> (i) was sent to the appellant; or
>> (ii) in a quality contracts scheme case, if the notice was not sent to the appellant, the date on which the notice was published in a newspaper in accordance with the requirement of section 125 (notice and consultation requirements) of the Transport Act 2000.".

It also inserted a new para.(7). Neither amendment affects social security cases and so the new para.(7) is not set out here.

p.1693, *amendments to the Tribunal Procedure (Upper Tribunal) Rules 2008 (SI 2008/2698) r.24 (Response to the notice of appeal)*

4.076 With effect from August 21, 2015, rr.2 and 5 of the Tribunal Procedure (Amendment) Rules 2015 (SI 2015/1510) inserted new paras (1)(ab) and (6). Neither amendment is relevant to social security cases and so they are not set out here.

p.1694, *amendments to the Tribunal Procedure (Upper Tribunal) Rules 2008 (SI 2008/2698) r.25 (Appellant's reply)*

4.077 With effect from August 21, 2015, rr.2 and 6 of the Tribunal Procedure (Amendment) Rules 2015 (SI 2015/1510) inserted new paras (2B) and (4). Neither amendment is relevant to social security cases and so they are not set out here.

p.1718, *insertion of the Tribunal Procedure (Upper Tribunal) Rules 2008 (SI 2008/2698) Sch.A1 (Procedure in quality contract scheme cases)*

4.078 With effect from August 21, 2015, rr.2 and 7 of the Tribunal Procedure (Amendment) Rules 2015 (SI 2015/1510) inserted a new Sch.A1 into the Rules. It is not relevant to social security cases and so is not set out here.

pp.1719–1720, *annotation to the Practice Direction (First-tier and Upper Tribunals: Children, Vulnerable Adults and Sensitive Witnesses)*

4.079 This Practice Direction still has not been revised. For its relevance to deciding whether to proceed with a hearing in a party's absence, see the annotation to r.31 of the Tribunal Procedure (First-tier Tribunal) (Social Entitlement Chamber) Rules 2008 in the main volume, as supplemented above.

In *JH(S) v SSWP (ESA)* [2015] UKUT 567 (AAC), it was suggested that defining "vulnerable adult" by reference to the definition in the Safeguarding Vulnerable Groups Act 2006 no longer made sense in the light of amendments to that Act.

PART V

UPDATING MATERIAL:
VOLUME IV

TAX CREDITS AND HMRC-
ADMINISTERED SOCIAL SECURITY
BENEFITS

Commentary by

Nick Wikeley

David Williams

Ian Hooker

p.xvii, *Using this Book—Northern Ireland legislation*

As mentioned in the main volume, the Welfare Reform and Work Bill that was intended to replicate in Northern Ireland most of the provisions of the Welfare Reform Act 2012 failed to pass its final stage in the Northern Ireland Assembly in May 2015 because it had not gained the necessary cross-community support. This had substantial budgetary implications because the United Kingdom Government funds welfare in Northern Ireland only up to the levels that apply in Great Britain and the 2012 Act had achieved a substantial reduction of expenditure in Great Britain. In consequence, there were 11 weeks of talks between the United Kingdom Government, Northern Ireland politicians and the Irish Government (under the approach required by the 1998 Belfast Agreement), leading to an agreement on November 17, 2015 which resulted in the Northern Ireland (Welfare Reform) Act 2015 being passed by the United Kingdom Parliament and receiving Royal Assent on November 25, 2015. It is a short statute, authorising the making of Orders in Council to make provision in connection with social security in Northern Ireland, provided that any such Order in Council is made by the end of 2016. The Welfare Reform (Northern Ireland) Order 2015 (SI 2015/2006) was duly made on December 9, 2015 and, by virtue of s.2 of the Act, is treated as an Act of the Northern Ireland Assembly. It is similar to the Bill that had failed in the Assembly seven months earlier. Most of the provisions in it will come into force in accordance with commencement orders made by the Department for Social Development. Northern Ireland legislation will then converge again with Great Britain legislation and, for instance, personal independence payment will be introduced in Northern Ireland.

p.9, *amendment to the Taxes Management Act 1970 s.9B (Amendment of return by taxpayer during enquiry)*

With effect from July 17, 2014, Sch.33, para.1 of the Finance Act 2014 amended s.9B(1) by inserting after "return by taxpayer" the following: "or in accordance with Chapter 2 of Part 4 of the Finance Act 2014 (amendment of return after follower notice". 5.001

p.15, *amendment to the Taxes Management Act 1970 s.36 (Loss of tax brought about carelessly or deliberately etc.)*

With effect from July 17, 2014, s.277(1) of the Finance Act 2014 amended s.36(1A) by adding at the end: 5.002

"or,
   (d) attributable to an arrangement that were expected to give rise to a tax advantage in respect of which the person was under an obligation to notify the Commissioners for Her Majesty's Revenue and Customs under section 253 of the Finance Act 2014 (duty to notify Commissioners of promoter reference number) but failed to do so."

p.33, *annotation to the Social Security Contributions and Benefits Act 1992 s.143 (Meaning of "person responsible for a child or qualifying young person")*

5.003   Where the claimant does not have the child living with them it must be shown that they are providing for the child "at a weekly rate which is not less than the weekly rate of child benefit".

The meaning of this phrase has been examined in a decision of Judge Knowles QC, *RK v HMRC* [2015] UKUT 357 AAC, to be reported as [2016] AACR 4. The claimant, living and working in the UK, but whose wife and children remained in Poland, had initially taken sums of money back to his family himself or sent them with friends who were returning; subsequently he made payments periodically through a money transfer system. The claim for Child Benefit was refused and an appeal to the FTT rejected on the ground that he had not contributed at the required rate. In the UT Judge Knowles found, on the evidence, that he had done so; the FTT were in error, she thought, because they had assumed that what the claimant had shown on his claim form as living expenses related only to himself (thereby leaving too little to have sent home to his family) whereas the claimant had included there the living expenses that he was providing for both himself and his wife. But although the representative of HMRC accepted that this did allow for contributions to have been made at the necessary rate they argued further, that the payments needed to have been made as weekly payments. The judge rejected that argument. She found nothing in this section, or in the Child Benefit (General) Regulations, to compel her to reach that conclusion and observed that, on the contrary, it would be inconvenient for persons who were paid at intervals greater than a week, or who were self-employed, if they had to budget the for those amounts and then pay them each week.

p.136, *additional note to the Tax Credits Act 2002 on repeal of the 2002 Act*

5.004   As at October 2015 a major roll-out of universal credit started, with a focus in particular on single claimants and therefore on those who could claim working tax credit rather than child tax credit. The extent of the roll-out is covered by Volume V of this work. A full up to date list of areas covered by universal credit, at least in part, can be found in the guidance at   *http://www.gov.uk/guidance/jobcentres-where-you-can-claim-universal-credit.* As an area is brought within universal credit, so entitlement to tax credits is abated.

p.139, *additional note following heading "Changes since enactment"*

5.005   The *HMRC Error and Fraud Statistics 2013–14* show a significant drop in errors to 4.4 per cent overpaid and 0.6 per cent underpaid. A major area of continuing error and fraud is considered by HMRC to be the issue of those who should be making joint claims but instead make claims as single individuals. The Chancellor announced a public consultation about such claims in the Autumn Statement 2015 (para.3.5).

Two sets of further major changes to the tax credits system were announced in 2015. The first is a major extension of the introduction of universal credit to replace tax credits, with the first additional stage of the extension taking place in October 2015. See the separate commentary on this in Vol.5 of this series.

The second set of changes was announced by the Chancellor of the Exchequer in the Summer Budget 2015 that followed the General Election. They together amounted to a significant trimming of the levels of entitlement of many tax credit claimants, with smaller groups obtaining an increased benefit. The main intended changes were published in 2015 as a draft statutory instrument, the draft *Tax Credits (Income Thresholds and Determination of Rates) (Amendment) Regulations*. However, following a series of defeats of the Government policy for tax credit changes in the House of Lords in October 2015, the Chancellor announced in the Autumn Statement 2015 in November that the Government were not proceeding with proposals to introduce those changes. The draft regulations were therefore not confirmed. Instead, the Chancellor announced that the reductions in entitlement would occur when tax credit claimants were to be transferred to universal credit. He also announced that any new claimant for tax credits from 2018 would instead be required to claim universal credit. This effectively means that, for new claimants, the abolition of the tax credits scheme will take place in that year. Current government proposals would transfer all other tax credit claimants to universal credit in 2020.

p.148, *additional note following heading "Subsections (5A), (6A)"*

Upper Tribunal judges have continued to criticise both HMRC and 5.006
decisions of the First-tier Tribunal concerning the question whether an individual should be claiming as one of a couple rather than as a single claimant. See in particular *NI v HMRC* [2015] UKUT 160 (AAC) where the Upper Tribunal criticised the approach of both the First-tier Tribunal and HMRC. In particular in that case the judge emphasised that there was no presumption in law that both the parents of children had shared responsibility for children where the parents were not married to each other. And in *TS v HMRC* [2015] UKUT 507 (AAC) the Upper Tribunal judge followed the recent decision of the Upper Tribunal in *DG v HMRC* [2013] UKUT 631 (AAC) but cautioned that tribunals should not put too much weight on the evidence of a "financial footprint" as compared with other evidence. In some cases the errors below are so clear that the Upper Tribunal, sometimes with the active support of HMRC, does not hesitate to reverse the decision of the First-tier Tribunal on the facts. See for a recent example *SW v HMRC* [2015] UKUT 394 (AAC).

Two linked recurring themes in Upper Tribunal decisions about whether someone is or is not a member of a couple are the question of the burden of proof and ensuring that a First-tier Tribunal has all the available evidence before it. See on that point the decision of the Upper Tribunal in *JW v HMRC* [2015] UKUT 369 (AAC). For a decision stressing that in any decision made under s.19 (power to enquire) the onus of proof is on HMRC not the claimant see *TS v HMRC* [2015] UKUT 507 (AAC).

More generally, HMRC is to undertake a public consultation about questions of error and fraud with respect to single claims in cases where it is contended that the claim should be a joint claim (Autumn Statement 2015).

p.178, *annotation to the Tax Credits Act 2002 s.19 (Power to enquire)*

5.007   In *TS v HMRC* [2015] UKUT 507 (AAC) the Upper Tribunal judge ruled that the burden of proof in an appeal against a decision of HMRC made under s.19 is on HMRC not the claimant. It is particularly important therefore in such cases that a tribunal considering an appeal ensures that it has all the relevant evidence before it, and in particular all evidence that a claimant has submitted to HMRC in response to its power to enquire. A s.19 enquiry must commence with notice to the person or persons making the claim under enquiry, so putting the claimant on notice to provide evidence. The section also empowers the requirement that evidence be produced. Any evidence so produced must be put before the tribunal on an appeal. Furthermore, it is the duty of the tribunal to ensure that this is done, as was emphasised by Judge Wright in *JW v HMRC* [2015] UKUT 369 (AAC). A failure to do this will be both a failure to comply with the Tribunal Rules and a breach of natural justice.

p.192, *annotation to the Tax Credits Act 2002 s.31 (Incorrect statements, etc)*

5.008   As regards the level of penalties, in *AP v HMRC* [2015] UKUT 580 (AAC), Judge Mark set aside a decision of the First-tier Tribunal on a penalty case because the tribunal had not dealt with the question adequately. In such a case it was for the tribunal itself to decide the level of penalty, not merely conduct a review exercise of the decision taken by HMRC. The tribunal must show that it has exercised a reasoned judicial discretion in making that decision.

p.194, *annotation to the Tax Credits Act 2002 s.32 (Failure to comply with requirements)*

5.009   See the additional note to s.31 with regard to the duty of tribunals in appeals about penalties.

p.206, *annotation to the Tax Credits Act 2002 s.38 (Appeals)*

5.010   The change of practice by HMRC with regard to the provision of full evidence and submissions to the First-tier Tribunal is noted and discussed by Judge Wright in *JW v HMRC* [2015] UKUT 369 (AAC). As he notes there, it is accepted by HMRC that templates used in the Tax Credit Office before May 2014 did not comply with relevant requirements. HMRC has now stopped the use of those templates and, more generally, revised its guidance to officials preparing submissions for tribunals. See HMRC *Tax Credits Manual* at TCM0014000. It follows that any submission made by the Tax Credits Office before then is likely to be non-compliant and should be questioned on any appeal.

pp.303–304, *amendments to the Child Trust Funds Act 2004 s.3 (Requirements to be satisfied)*

With effect from May 26, 2015, s.61(2) of the Deregulation Act 2015 amended subs.(6) by substituting for paras (a) and (b) the following— 5.011

> "(a) if the child is 16 or over and has elected to manage the child trust fund, is the child;
> (b) in any other case, is the person who has that authority by virtue of subsection (7) (but subject to subsection (10))."

With effect from the same date, ss.61(3) and (4) of the same Act also omitted "under 16" in subs.(8) (where it first occurs) and in subs.(10).

With effect from May 26, 2015, s.60(2) of the Deregulation Act 2015 amended subs.(10) by substituting "is to be a person appointed by the Treasury or by the Secretary of State" for the words from "is to be" to the end of the subsection. With effect from the same date, s.60(3) of the same Act inserted after subs.(11) the following new sub-sections:

> "(11A) Regulations under subsection (10) may provide that, where the terms on which a person is appointed by the Treasury or by the Secretary of State include provision for payment to the person, the payment must be made by a government department specified in the regulations (instead of by the person making the appointment).
>
> (11B) Regulations may provide that, where a person authorised to manage a child trust fund by virtue of subsection (10) ceases to be so authorised, the person must provide any information held by that person in connection with the management of the fund to the person (if any) who becomes authorised by virtue of that subsection to manage the trust fund instead."

p.321, *amendments to the Child Trust Funds Act 2004 s.16 (Information about children in care of authority)*

With effect from May 26, 2015, s.60(4) of the Deregulation Act 2015 amended subs.(1) by inserting "or by a person appointed under regulations under section 3(10)" at the end of para.(a) (before ", or"), by inserting "or to such a person" before "any information" in para.(b) and by inserting "or (as the case may be) the person" before "may require" in the words following para.(b). 5.012

p.506, *amendment to the Tax Credits (Definition and Calculation of Income) Regulations 2002 (SI 2002/2006), reg.19, Table 6 (Sums disregarded in the calculation of income)*

With effect from April 1, 2014, art.2 and para.8 of the Sch. to the Social Care (Self-directed Support) (Scotland) Act 2013 (Consequential 5.012.1

Modifications and Savings) Order 2014 (SI 2014/513) amended para.14 of Table 6 so as to omit "section 12B of the Social Work (Scotland) Act 1968" and to insert after "2002" the phrase "or as a direct payment as defined in section 4(2) of the Social Care (Self-directed Support) (Scotland) Act 2013".

p.645, *amendment to the Child Benefit (General) Regulations 2006 (SI 2006/223) reg.1 (Citation, commencement and interpretation)*

5.013   With effect from August 31, 2015, the Child Benefit (General) (Amendment) Regulations 2015 (SI 2015/1512) reg.2 amends reg.1(3) as follows:

"(a) omit sub-paragraph (a); and
(b) in sub-paragraph (d), after "known as", insert ""United Youth Pilot","."

p.649, *annotation to the Child Benefit (General) Regulations 2006 (SI 2006/223) reg.3 (Education and training condition)*

5.014   In *JH v HMRC* [2015] UKUT 479 AAC Judge Levenson has decided an unusual case affecting a young person who was the subject of a special educational needs statement. He was educated at a special school until the age of 18 and then at home under an arrangement made by his local authority. His mother's claim for Child Benefit to be continued under this regulation was, however, refused because under reg.3(3) such a course of training could only be approved if it had commenced whilst he was still a child (i.e. under the age of 16). Judge Levenson allowed an appeal on grounds that had been agreed between the parties; the limitation in reg.3(3) was found only in secondary legislation. This meant that it should be disapplied if it were found to be in breach of the claimant's rights under the Human Rights Act 1998. The judge found that the unequal treatment between claimants whose child began home education under the age of 16 and those whose child was older, was a breach of the claimant's Convention rights under art.14 and art.1 and could not be justified.

p.999, *amendments to the Child Trust Funds Regulations 2004 (SI 2004/1450) reg.2 (Interpretation)*

5.015   With effect from July 1, 2015, reg.2 of the Child Trust Funds (Amendment No.3) Regulations 2015 (SI 2015/1371) amended reg.2(1)(a) by omitting the words ", in relation to a child under 16" in the definition of "responsible person".

p.1000, *amendments to the Child Trust Funds Regulations 2004 (SI 2004/1450) reg.2 (Interpretation)*

5.016   With effect from July 1, 2015, reg.4(1)(a) of the Child Trust Funds (Amendment No.3) Regulations 2015 (SI 2015/1371) amended the definition of "company" in reg.2(1)(b) by inserting "or" at the end of para.(i), substituting a semicolon for the comma at the end of para.(ii) and omitting paras (iii) and (iv).

p.1002, *amendments to the Child Trust Funds Regulations 2004 (SI 2004/1450) reg.2 (interpretation)*

With effect from July 1, 2015, reg.4(1)(b) and (c) of the Child Trust Funds (Amendment No.3) Regulations 2015 (SI 2015/1371) amended reg.2(1)(b) by omitting the definition of "registered society" and by inserting after the definition of "recognised stock exchange" the following new definition— **5.017**

""registered contact" means the person who has the authority to manage the child trust fund by virtue of section 3(6) of the Act;".

p.1005, *amendments to the Child Trust Funds Regulations 2004 (SI 2004/1450) reg.2 (Interpretation)*

With effect from July 1, 2015, reg.4(2) of the Child Trust Funds (Amendment No.3) Regulations 2015 (SI 2015/1371) amended reg.2(2) by omitting the entry for "registered contact" in the table. **5.018**

p.1013, *amendments to the Child Trust Funds Regulations 2004 (SI 2004/1450) reg.8 (General requirements for accounts)*

With effect from July 1, 2015, reg.5 of the Child Trust Funds (Amendment No.3) Regulations 2015 (SI 2015/1371) amended reg.8 by omitting sub-para.(1)(d) (registered contact). **5.019**

p.1021, *amendments to the Child Trust Funds Regulations 2004 (SI 2004/1450) reg.12 (Qualifying investments for an account)*

With effect from July 1, 2015, reg.6 of the Child Trust Funds (Amendment No.3) Regulations 2015 (SI 2015/1371) amended reg.12(5) by substituting a semicolon at the end of sub-para.(c) for the full stop and, after that sub-paragraph, inserting the following new sub-paragraphs— **5.020**

"(d) that the shares in the company issuing the securities are admitted to trading on a recognised stock exchange in the European Economic Area;
(e) that the securities are so admitted to trading;
(f) that the company issuing the securities is a 75 per cent subsidiary of a company whose shares are so admitted to trading."

p.1024–1025, *amendments to the Child Trust Funds Regulations 2004 (SI 2004/1450) reg.13 (Conditions for application by responsible person or the child to open an account (and changes to an account))*

With effect from July 1, 2015, reg.7 of the Child Trust Funds (Amendment No.3) Regulations 2015 (SI 2015/1371) amended **5.021** reg.13(10)(b) by substituting for the words "and a responsible" to the end the following—

"and —
  (i) a responsible person in relation to the child subsequently applies to the account provider to be the registered contact for the account, or
  (ii) the child, if the child is 16 or over and has elected to manage the account, subsequently applies to the account provider to be the registered contact for the account,

that individual must make the application or declaration required by paragraphs (3) to (5) but as if for regulation 13(3)(b) there were substituted—

"(b) is—
  (i) a responsible person in relation to the named child (that is, that he has parental responsibility or, in Scotland, parental responsibilities in relation to the child), or
  (ii) the child, where the child is 16 or over and has elected to manage the account.""

p.1034, *amendments to the Child Trust Funds Regulations 2004 (SI 2004/1450) reg.13 (Transfers of accounts)*

5.022   With effect from July 1, 2015, reg.8 of the Child Trust Funds (Amendment No.3) Regulations 2015 (SI 2015/1371) amended reg.21(3) by adding at the end add "but (in the case mentioned in sub-paragraph (b)) as if for regulation 13(3)(b) there were substituted—

"(b) is—
  (i) a responsible person in relation to the named child (that is, that he has parental responsibility or, in Scotland, parental responsibilities in relation to the child, or
  (ii) the child, where the child is 16 or over and has elected to manage the account."

p.1044, *amendments to the Child Trust Funds Regulations 2004 (SI 2004/1450) reg.33A (The Official Solicitor or Accountant of Court to be the person who has the authority to manage an account)*

5.023   With effect from July 1, 2015, reg.9(a) of the Child Trust Funds (Amendment No.3) Regulations 2015 (SI 2015/1371) amended reg.33A(1)(a)(ii) by substituting "18" for "16".

p.1047, *amendments to the Child Trust Funds Regulations 2004 (SI 2004/1450) reg.33A (the Official Solicitor or Accountant of Court to be the person who has the authority to manage an account)*

5.024   With effect from July 1, 2015, reg.9(b)-(d) of the Child Trust Funds (Amendment No.3) Regulations 2015 (SI 2015/1371) amended para.(4)(a) by substituting "is 16 or over and has elected to manage the account" for "attains the age of 16", and by omitting "under 16 and still" in para.(4)(b) and "is under 16 and" in para.(4)(c).

PART VI

FORTHCOMING CHANGES AND UP-RATINGS OF BENEFITS

FORTHCOMING CHANGES

REGULATIONS

Social Security (Housing Costs Amendments) Regulations 2015

The Social Security (Housing Costs Amendments) Regulations 2015 **6.001** (SI 2015/1647) come into force on April 1, 2016. They amend the Income Support (General) Regulations 1987 (SI 1987/1967), the Jobseeker's Allowance Regulations 1996 (SI 1996/207), the Employment and Support Allowance Regulations 2008 (SI 2008/794) and the Universal Credit Regulations 2013 (SI 2013/376) so that, in respect of a new claim for any of these benefits made on or after April 1, 2016 (that does not link to a previous claim), the waiting period for housing costs will be 39 weeks (9 assessment periods in the case of universal credit).

Since October 1995 the waiting period for "full" housing costs has been 26 weeks in the case of "existing housing costs" and 39 weeks in the case of "new housing costs" but this was changed to 13 weeks for certain claimants with effect from January 5, 2009 by the Social Security (Housing Costs Special Arrangements) (Amendment and Modification) Regulations 2008 (SI 2008/3195) (those Regulations were themselves further amended on January 5, 2010).

The provisions in the 2008 Regulations that modified the waiting period are revoked, subject to a saving provision for claimants who are in a waiting period for housing costs on March 31, 2016. The effect of the saving provision is that for those claimants who are entitled, or treated as entitled, to income support, jobseeker's allowance, employment and support allowance or universal credit for a period which includes March 31, 2016, the modifications made to Sch.3 to the Income Support (General) Regulations 1987, Sch.2 to the Jobseeker's Allowance Regulations 1996 and Sch.6 to the Employment and Support Allowance Regulations 2008 by the 2008 Regulations continue to have effect and the amendments made to Sch.5 to the Universal Credit Regulations 2013 by the 2015 Regulations do not apply. In other words, for such claimants the waiting period for housing costs remains 13 weeks.

The 2008 Regulations also modified the Income Support (General) **6.002** Regulations 1987, the Jobseeker's Allowance Regulations 1996 and the Employment and Support Allowance Regulations 2008 by increasing the ceiling on loans from £100,000 to £200,000. In addition, in the case of jobseeker's allowance only, housing costs in respect of eligible loans are only payable for two years. These modifications continue for those claimants to whom the 2008 Regulations apply, as does the modification relating to claimants of state pension credit. For further discussion of these modifications, see the notes to Sch.3 to the Income Support (General) Regulations 1987 in Vol.II of this series.

Various consequential amendments are also made to the Income Support (General) Regulations 1987, the Jobseeker's Allowance Regulations 1996 and the Employment and Support Allowance Regulations 2008 as a result of the abolition of the distinction between "new" and "existing" housing costs. In addition, para.7 of Sch.3 to the Income Support (General) Regulations 1987 (which provided transitional protection on the introduction of the October 1995 changes to housing costs) is revoked.

The Explanatory Memorandum which accompanies this SI states that the 13 week waiting period was part of a package of temporary measures introduced to support homeowners and the housing industry during the recession. However, "[a]s the housing and labour markets have now recovered, the Government has decided that it is the right time to re-introduce a 39 week waiting period for new claims".

NEW BENEFIT RATES FROM APRIL 2016

NEW BENEFIT RATES FROM APRIL 2014

(Benefits covered in Volume I)

	April 2015	April 2016
	£ pw	£ pw
Disability benefits		
Attendance allowance		
higher rate	82.30	82.30
lower rate	55.10	55.10
Disability living allowance		
care component		
highest rate	82.30	82.30
middle rate	55.10	55.10
lowest rate	21.80	21.80
mobility component		
higher rate	57.45	57.45
lower rate	21.80	21.80
Personal independence payment		
daily living component		
enhanced rate	82.30	82.30
standard rate	55.10	55.10
mobility component		
enhanced rate	57.45	57.45
standard rate	21.80	21.80
Carer's allowance	62.10	62.10
Severe disablement allowance		
basic rate	74.65	74.65
age related addition—higher rate	11.15	11.15
age related addition—middle rate	6.20	6.20
age related addition—lower rate	6.20	6.20

New Benefit Rates from April 2016

	April 2015 £ pw	April 2016 £ pw
Maternity benefits		
Maternity allowance		
standard rate	139.58	139.58
Bereavement benefits and retirement pensions		
Widowed parent's allowance or widowed mother's allowance	112.55	112.55
Bereavement allowance or widow's pension		
standard rate	112.55	112.55
Retirement pension		
Category A	115.95	119.30
Category B (higher)	115.95	119.30
Category B (lower)	69.50	71.50
Category C	69.50	71.50
Category D	69.50	71.50
New state pension	—	155.65
Incapacity benefit		
Long-term incapacity benefit		
basic rate	105.35	105.35
increase for age—higher rate	11.15	11.15
increase for age—lower rate	6.20	6.20
invalidity allowance—higher rate	11.15	11.15
invalidity allowance—middle rate	6.20	6.20
invalidity allowance—lower rate	6.20	6.20
Short-term incapacity benefit		
under pension age—higher rate	94.05	94.05
under pension age—lower rate	79.45	79.45
over pension age—higher rate	105.35	105.35
over pension age—lower rate	101.10	101.10
Dependency increases		
Adult		
carer's allowance	36.75	36.75
severe disablement allowance	36.55	36.55
retirement pension	65.70	65.70
long-term incapacity benefit	61.20	61.20
short-term incapacity benefit under pension age	47.65	47.65
short-term incapacity benefit over pension age	58.90	58.90
Child	11.35[1]	11.35[1]

	April 2015	April 2016
	£ pw	£ pw

Industrial injuries benefits

Disablement benefit

100%	168.00	168.00
90%	151.20	151.20
80%	134.40	134.40
70%	117.60	117.60
60%	100.80	100.80
50%	84.00	84.00
40%	67.20	67.20
30%	50.40	50.40
20%	33.60	33.60

unemployability supplement

basic rate	103.85	103.85
increase for adult dependant	61.20	61.20
increase for child dependant	11.35[1]	11.35[1]
increase for early incapacity—higher rate	21.50	21.50
increase for early incapacity—middle rate	13.90	13.90
increase for early incapacity—lower rate	6.95	6.95

constant attendance allowance

exceptional rate	134.40	134.40
intermediate rate	100.80	100.80
normal maximum rate	67.30	67.20
part-time rate	33.60	33.60

exceptionally severe disablement allowance	67.20	67.20

Reduced earnings allowance

maximum rate	67.20	67.20

Death benefit
widow's pension

higher rate	115.95	119.30
lower rate	34.79	35.79
widower's pension	115.95	119.30

Notes

1. These sums payable in respect of children are reduced if payable in respect of the only, elder or eldest child for whom child benefit is being paid (see reg.8 of the Social Security (Overlapping Benefits) Regulations 1979 on p.600 of Vol. 1 of the main work).

	April 2015 £ pw	April 2016 £ pw
Employment and support allowance		
Contribution-based personal rates		
assessment phase—*aged under 25*	57.90	57.90
aged 25 or over	73.10	73.10
main phase	73.10	73.10
Components		
work-related activity	29.05	29.05
support	36.20	36.20
Income-based personal allowances		
single person—*aged under 25*	57.90	57.90
aged 25 or over	73.10	73.10
lone parent—*aged under 18*	57.90	57.90
aged 18 or over	73.10	73.10
couple—*both aged under 18*	57.90	57.90
both aged under 18, with a child	87.50	87.50
both aged under 18, (main phase)	73.10	73.10
both aged under 18, with a child (main phase)	114.85	114.85
one aged under 18, one aged 18 or over	114.85	114.85
both aged 18 or over	114.85	114.85
Premiums		
pensioner—*single person with no component*	78.10	82.50
couple with no component	116.00	122.70
enhanced disability—*single person*	15.75	15.75
couple	22.60	22.60
severe disability—*single person*	61.85	61.85
couple (one qualifies)	61.85	61.85
couple (both qualify)	123.70	123.70
carer	34.60	34.60

NEW BENEFIT RATES FROM APRIL 2016

(Benefits covered in Volume II)

	April 2015	April 2016
	£ pw	£ pw
Contribution-based jobseeker's allowance		
personal rates—*aged under 25*	57.90	57.90
aged 25 or over	73.10	73.10
Income support and income-based jobseeker's allowance		
personal allowances		
single person—*aged under 25*	57.90	57.90
aged 25 or over	73.10	73.10
lone parent—*aged under 18*	57.90	57.90
aged 18 or over	73.10	73.10
couple—*both aged under 18*	57.90	57.90
both aged under 18, with a child	87.50	87.50
one aged under 18, one aged under 25	57.90	57.90
one aged under 18, one aged 25 or over	73.10	73.10
both aged 18 or over	114.85	114.85
child	66.90	66.90
premiums		
family—*ordinary*	17.45	17.45
lone parent	17.45	17.45
pensioner—*single person (JSA only)*	78.10	82.50
couple	116.00	122.70
disability—*single person*	32.25	32.25
couple	45.95	45.95
enhanced disability—*single person*	15.75	15.75
couple	22.60	22.60
disabled child	24.43	24.43
severe disability—*single person*	61.85	61.85
couple (one qualifies)	61.85	61.85
couple (both qualify)	123.70	123.70
disabled child	60.06	60.06
carer	34.60	34.60
Pension credit		
Standard minimum guarantee		
single person	151.20	155.60
couple	230.85	237.55

New Benefit Rates from April 2016

	April 2015 £ pw	April 2016 £ pw
Additional amount for severe disability		
single person	61.85	61.85
couple (one qualifies)	61.85	61.85
couple (both qualify)	123.70	123.70
Additional amount for carers	34.60	34.60
Savings credit threshold		
single person	126.50	133.82
couple	201.80	201.80
Maximum savings credit		
single person	14.82	13.07
couple	17.43	14.75

NEW TAX CREDIT AND BENEFIT RATES 2016–2017

(Benefits covered in Volume IV)

	2015–16	2016–17
	£ pw	£ pw
Benefits in respect of children		
Child benefit		
only, elder or eldest child (couple)	20.70	20.70
each subsequent child	13.70	13.70
Guardian's allowance	16.55	16.55
Employer-paid benefits		
Standard rates		
Statutory sick pay	88.45	88.45
Statutory maternity pay	139.58	139.58
Statutory paternity pay	139.58	139.58
Statutory adoption pay	139.58	139.58
Income threshold	112.00	112.00

	2015–16	2016–17
	£ pa	£ pa
Working tax credit		
Basic element	1,960	1,960
Couple and lone parent element	2,010	2,010
30 hour element	810	810
Disabled worker element	2,970	2,970
Severe disability element	1,275	1,275
Child care element		
maximum eligible cost for one child	*175 pw*	*175 pw*
maximum eligible cost for two or more		
children	*300 pw*	*300 pw*
per cent of eligible costs covered	*70%*	*70%*
Child tax credit		
Family element	545	545
Child element	2,780	2,780
Disabled child element	3,140	3,140
Severely disabled child element	1,275	1,275
Tax credit income thresholds		
Income rise disregard	5,000	2,500
Income fall disregard	2,500	2,500
Income threshold	6,420	6,420
Income threshold for those entitled to child tax		
credit only	16,105	16,105
Withdrawal rate	*41%*	*41%*

NEW UNIVERSAL CREDIT RATES FROM APRIL 2016

(Benefits covered in Volume V)

	April 2015	April 2016
	£ pw	£ pw
Standard allowances		
Single claimant—*aged under 25*	251.77	251.77
aged 25 or over	317.82	317.82
Joint claimant—*both aged under 25*	395.20	395.20
one or both aged 25 or over	498.89	498.89
Child element—*first child*	277.08	277.08
second/ subsequent child	231.67	231.67
Disabled child addition—*lower rate*	126.11	126.11
higher rate	367.92	367.92
Limited Capability for Work element	126.11	126.11
Limited Capability for Work and Work-Related Activity element	315.60	315.60
Carer element	150.39	150.39
Childcare element—*maximum for one child*	532.29	532.29
maximum for two or more children	912.50	1,108.04
Non-dependants' housing cost contributions	69.37	69.37
Work allowances		
Higher work allowance (no housing element)		
Single claimant—*no dependent children*	111.00	nil
one or more children	734.00	397.00
limited capability for work	647.00	397.00
Joint claimant—*no dependent children*	111.00	nil
one or more children	536.00	397.00
limited capability for work	647.00	397.00
Lower work allowance		
Single claimant—*no dependent children*	111.00	nil
one or more children	263.00	192.00
limited capability for work	192.00	192.00
Joint claimant—*no dependent children*	111.00	nil
one or more children	222.00	192.00
limited capability for work	192.00	192.00